MW00439476

Following the Royal Road

Opening the Camino Real by Ron Kil

Following the Royal Road

A Guide to the Historic Camino Real de Tierra Adentro

Hal Jackson

Foreword by Marc Simmons

University of New Mexico Press + Albuquerque

20 19 18 17 16 15   3 4 5 6 7 8

Library of Congress Cataloging-in-Publication Data

Jackson, Hal (Hal E.)
Following the Royal Road : a guide to the historic
Camino Real de Tierra Adentro / Hal Jackson.
p. cm.
Includes bibliographical references and index.
ISBN-13: 978-0-8263-4085-6 (pbk. : alk. paper)
ISBN-10: 0-8263-4085-7 (pbk. : alk. paper)
1. El Camino Real de Tierra Adentro
National Historic Trail (N.M. and Tex.)—Guidebooks.
I. Title.
F802.E45J33 2006
978.9—dc22

2006017250

All maps created by Hal Jackson
Frontispiece and chapter start illustration by Ron Kil
Cover and book design by Kathleen Sparkes
This book is typeset using Minion 12/15, 31p
Display type is Serlio and Arcana Standard Manuscript

In loving memory

of my daughter,

LAURA DIANE JACKSON

Contents

Maps

Sidebars

✝ x ✝

Foreword

The book you hold in your hand is the first motorists' guide to the historic Camino Real. As initially completed in 1598, this "Royal Road" ran south from New Mexico's San Juan Pueblo four hundred miles to the El Paso Valley, thence continued onward by way of desert uplands and mining settlements, to reach at last Mexico City, the viceregal capital of the colony of New Spain.

People there, according to scientist and world traveler Alexander von Humboldt, commonly spoke of this lengthy thoroughfare stretching northward as "El Camino Real de Tierra Adentro," that is, "The Road from the Interior." The last word referred to the interior of the viceroyalty, which was also at the interior of the continent. Other *caminos reales*, or government roads, forked off from the main artery, Mexico City to New Mexico. One of those branches reached Spanish Texas by the end of the seventeenth century, and another in the last quarter of the eighteenth century veered northwestward through Sonora to serve the new missions and settlements of Upper California.

Guide author Hal Jackson, a professional geographer as well as a grassroots historian dedicated to defining old trails, has given us in the present work a comprehensive handbook. It will well serve modern-day explorers wishing to follow in the footsteps of conquistadors, Franciscan padres, soldiers, royal officials, pioneering Hispanic families, and finally merchantmen—Spanish, Mexican, and American.

Much of the guide's text is based on Jackson's firsthand explorations and observations of the Camino Real route. During the course of the writing, he made four complete round-trips from upper New Mexico to Mexico City. As necessary, he undertook additional short travels over individual segments of the road where serious detective work was required to locate elusive sites.

The book also leans heavily on surviving accounts of early-day travelers, beginning with New Mexico's founder, don Juan de Oñate, who blazed the last portion of the Camino Real from Santa Barbara in lower Chihuahua to New Mexico's San Juan Pueblo. Weight is given to the writings of such observant chroniclers as Rivera, Tamarón, Lafora, Pike, Gregg, Ruxton, Magoffin, and Webb. These chroniclers' quotes help to convey the atmosphere and spirit in which the overland traffic evolved during more than two-and-a-half centuries.

Hal Jackson believes that the sweetest part of the historic trail today lies in Mexico, where American tourists are least apt to follow it. To lure them south of the border, he has borne down on that section of the Camino Real extending from Oñate's hometown of Zacatecas northward across the central plateau and over the Chihuahuan desert to El Paso. Here can be found well-preserved landmarks dating from colonial days, as well as landscapes that appear much as they did long ago when viewed by passersby on horseback or in ox carts.

Recent years have seen a flurry of activity involving preservation, marking, and interpretation of El Camino Real de Tierra Adentro. In 1998, the United States and Mexico signed an agreement to cooperate in its conservation and management. The same year, the Federal Highway Administration designated the Camino Real as a National Scenic Byway.

In October 2000, the U.S. Congress established El Camino Real de Tierra Adentro National Historic Trail, administered jointly by the Department of Interior's National Park Service and the Bureau of Land Management in cooperation with federal, state, and local agencies and private landowners. This was the first international trail included under the National Trails Systems Act. United States jurisdiction reaches only to the Mexican border at El Paso, Texas.

Another significant development was the opening and dedication of El Camino Real International Heritage Center on November 19, 2005. Situated on the edge of a mesa overlooking the Rio Grande, the center lies thirty-five miles south of Socorro, New Mexico, off Interstate 25. Its exhibits, prepared in collaboration with Mexico's Instituto Nacional de Antropología e Historia, programs, desert gardens, and hiking trails commemorate and interpret the dramatic history of the Camino Real. The Museum of New Mexico, State Monuments Division, built the Heritage Center on 120 acres of public lands deeded by the federal Bureau of Land Management to the state of New Mexico in 2002. The facility became the sixth State Monument.

Finally, history-minded aficionados in 2003 organized El Camino Real de Tierra Adentro Trail Association (CARTA). Its aim is to promote the history and preservation of the old road. An informative journal, *Chronicles of the Trail*, is published quarterly. Membership information can be obtained from CARTA, PO Box 15162, Las Cruces, NM, 88004-5162.

It is clear that the Camino Real, after a long period of neglect, has now come into its own. Hal Jackson's guide should help innumerable travelers seek out and find the pleasures preserved in its historical riches.

—*Marc Simmons*
Cerillos, New Mexico

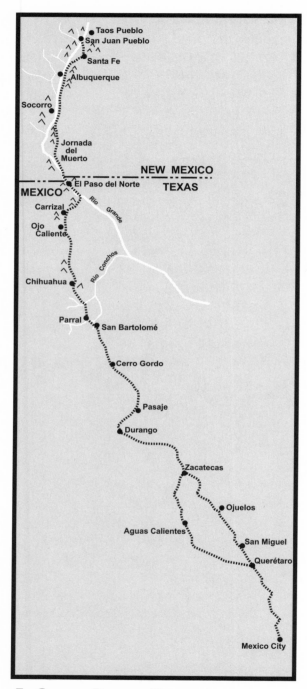

EL CAMINO REAL DE TIERRA ADENTRO

Preface

This book was written as a direct result of a suggestion by my good friend Harry Myers of the National Park Service. Harry knew that I had recently completed a revision of Marc Simmons's book *Following the Santa Fe Trail*, and we both knew that there was no guide to the Camino Real de Tierra Adentro (Royal Road of the Interior Land) but that public interest in this route is certain to increase, since the camino—at least those sections in the United States—was designated a National Historic Trail in 2000. Indeed, the Camino Real Trail Association, formed in 2003, has sponsored a series of meetings celebrating the camino. Another sign of interest is the opening of the Camino Real Heritage Center in a beautiful new building thirty-five miles south of Socorro, New Mexico. Although many caminos reales can be found in Mexico and the United States, the focus of this book is the camino from Mexico City into New Mexico.

The story of the Camino Real de Tierra Adentro should begin with the city of Zacatecas, the first toehold of the Spanish in La Gran Chichimeca, the large area that lay north of the region settled by sedentary agricultural Indians, since the silver strike at Zacatecas in 1546 provided the impetus for all settlement in northern Mexico. The founding of Zacatecas was what historian Philip Wayne Powell called "a pregnant historical moment." How many volunteers would Juan de Oñate have been able to enlist for his expedition to the north in 1598 without the hope of another Zacatecas? How would any expedition have been funded without the deep pockets of the mining families of Zacatecas? Religious fervor was an important element in the Spanish development of sixteenth-century Mexico, but the opportunity for riches was even more compelling for most.

North of Guadalajara and Querétaro lay the Gran Chichimeca, the area inhabited by several aggressive seminomadic hunting and gathering tribes. The Indians here fought valiantly to maintain their independence and were determined not to be forced into laboring for the Spaniards, who had to bring Indian and black slave labor north with them to provide workers for the mining communities dotting the landscape from Zacatecas to Santa Bárbara in what today is the state of Chihuahua. To protect these communities and the commerce of the Camino Real, the Spanish employed a strategy of siting small presidios, forts armed with a dozen soldiers, along the camino. Many of these presidios developed into small towns that one can visit today.

The primary struggle of the Spanish against the Chichimecas lasted from 1550 to 1600, concurrently with the construction of the silver camino from Zacatecas to Querétaro. Although they won control of this region, the Spanish continued to struggle against the Indians of the north throughout the colonial period. The successor political state, Mexico, inherited the struggle, battling Apache and Comanche warriors until after 1850.

The Camino Real was extended north with amazing speed. It took only seventy-seven years from the Spanish conquest of Tenochtitlán in 1521 until Juan de Oñate established a capital in New Mexico in 1598. If this accomplishment is compared with the glacial pace of English settlement westward from the Atlantic seaboard, the difference is striking. Ultimately the Camino Real de Tierra Adentro became the longest highway in North America, stretching fifteen hundred miles from Mexico City to northern New Mexico.

Traffic on the Camino Real in the seventeenth century was controlled by the Franciscan missionaries until the Pueblo Revolt in 1680 severed the northern portion of the camino at today's El Paso, Texas. Then, when Diego de Vargas reoccupied New Mexico in 1694, the Camino Real was reestablished as far north as Taos. Eighteenth-century trade on the Camino Real consisted principally of supplying the numerous mining communities in northern Mexico and transporting their silver south to Mexico City. Important silver ore discoveries had been made at Fresnillo and Sombrerete between Zacatecas and Durango and later at Parral and Santa Eulalia (now Aquiles Serdán) in Chihuahua. North of Chihuahua, traders carried basic materials for the small, agricultural population in New Mexico, where there were no major mines.

The most dramatic change to Camino Real trade occurred in 1821 with the independence of Mexico and the opening of the Santa Fe Trail from Missouri to New Mexico. The road was renamed the Camino Nacional by the Mexicans, and traffic increased on the section between Santa Fe and Chihuahua since American and Mexican traders were bringing commercial goods from Missouri to Santa Fe, where most of those commodities were then sent on to Chihuahua and beyond.

The northern section of the camino became known as the Chihuahua Trail. Beginning with Zebulon Pike's trip south on the Camino Real in 1807 (his journal was published in 1810) and followed by Josiah Gregg and others after 1821, Americans came to know a great deal about the northern part of the camino. Pike had passed south as a prisoner of the Spaniards; Gregg was a Santa Fe trader who published the most important book on the trails, *Commerce of the Prairies*. The war between Mexico and the United States in 1846–48 brought even more Americans to this area, who told their story in many wartime journals.

By following the directions in this guide, you can travel the historic Camino Real from Santa Fe to Mexico City. To help you find your way, sixty maps are included, and the many sidebars that provide additional information will broaden your understanding of the camino. Your trip will be more interesting if you read some background material before setting out (see the Suggested Readings section at the back of the book). An appendix contains travel information for those venturing into Mexico. This information will not substitute for a commercial travel book but lists locations that I used in many trips along the camino.

I am indebted to many people who helped me find my way along the Camino Real. In particular, I thank Harry Myers of the National Park Service for nudging me into this venture and Marc Simmons, who gave me strong encouragement along the way as well as valuable advice. Charlie Haecker, another Park Service expert, told me about his research on the Mexican War battle site at Brazito. Ben Brown took me by the hand in Chihuahua, showing me the presidio at Carrizal, and our friend George Turok was very helpful in El Paso, Texas. I am also indebted to Nick Houser in Ciudad Juárez and El Paso for guidance to the Pueblo Indian communities of that area. Rob Schmidt, a good friend for many years, drove south to Santa Bárbara with me. In Las Cruces, John and Jo Bloom introduced me to Charlotte Priestley, who owns the land near Fort Fillmore and knows that area well. In northern New Mexico, Peter Mackaness of Taos was very helpful, as was Herman Agoyo at San Juan Pueblo, who showed me old San Gabriel. In Santa Fe, Tom Bové showed me his beloved acequia and explained its history and workings. In La Ciénega, New Mexico, Archie Perea went with Marc Simmons and me to see that valley which Archie knows so well.

Martha and Joe Liebert of Bernalillo took time out of their lives to take me around that important area. David Jones of Placitas made several trips with me and provided valuable help. John Roney of the Bureau of Land Management in Albuquerque and Mike Marshall of Corrales spent time with me sharing their considerable research in Chihuahua and New Mexico. Art Howard took me from San Juan Pueblo to Las Cruces in his airplane for a fine view of the camino from the air. In the Albuquerque area, Ed Boles and Ben Moffet were both of great help. A special thanks goes to Michael and Pat Macklin for their joining me on the walk through the Río Santa Fe canyon, seeking the camino there. Of my many guides in Mexico, I will name only a few: in Chihuahua, Luís Urias; at the Sacramento battleground, guide/musician Jesús Neri Pacheco Chariva, who showed us the sites and also serenaded us at the battle site; in San Bartolomé, Rita Soto, the town's historian; in Cerrogordo, Sr. Gumaro, who showed us the camino in front of his house; and in Pánuco, Oñate's town, Edilberto Maldonado, who showed me the Oñate hacienda site.

I am greatly indebted to Rachel Snyder, who accompanied me to Zacatecas and wrote a very fine article for *American Heritage* on the Camino Real (May 2004). Ila Little edited the text for me, and I appreciate her help and attention to detail.

Charles Little was of great help to me when I needed him, and I appreciate his support. Finally, my thanks go to Leo Oliva, who spent many hours going over drafts of this book and traveling to Mexico with me. I could not have done it without Leo's help. A special thanks to two of my colleagues at the University of New Mexico, Elinore Barrett and Frank Pucci.

The maps and photos included here are mine except where noted. For most of my base maps, I utilized the U.S. Geological Survey (USGS) or, in Mexico, the Instituto Nacional de Estadística Geografía Informática (INEGI).

I know that a guidebook is expected to provide accurate numbers of the highways mentioned. Every time I traveled into Mexico, however, some highway numbers had been changed, and on my last visit, many numbers had been painted out. The Mexican government seems to be getting ready for a renumbering of highways. For that reason, be cautious when using numbers I provide. Still, the maps should be clear enough that you can work your way around these difficulties.

CHAPTER ONE

Santa Fe and the North

SANTA FE

Santa Fe, which bills itself as the "City Different," was settled in 1610 and has a remarkably long history. The descriptions here will focus on the Santa Fe of the colonial period, leaving the reader to seek out other guides (and there are many) for more recent times.

The city was sited in 1609 or 1610, and we can assume there was a formal plan for it, although one has never been found. We can guess what the plan spelled out since rules in play at that time were dictated in great detail by the Laws of the Indies. Most cities in the New World followed the dictates of these laws, with exceptions made for mining towns that grew so quickly with sites so challenging that there was no time to make a formal plan. (You will visit Zacatecas and Guanajuato, two good examples of such unplanned cities.)

The plans followed several "rules." First, the city would be laid out on a grid—two sets of streets at right angles to each other. The grid was to be tilted one-eighth turn from north-south. The Spaniards felt this shifting away from north-south kept disagreeable winds out of the city. Further, the plaza would be identified in anticipation of the city's expected importance. A city that was designated the capital of a province, as Santa Fe was, would have had a very large plaza prescribed.

PLAN OF SANTA FE

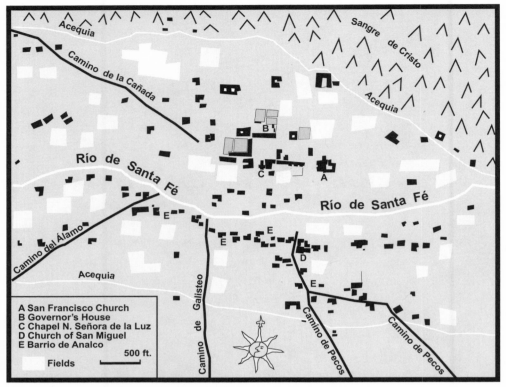

A San Francisco Church
B Governor's House
C Chapel N. Señora de la Luz
D Church of San Miguel
E Barrio de Analco

500 ft.

Fields

Based on a map drawn by Joseph de Urrutia in 1766

Facing the plaza, again as written into the laws, would be the seat of government (governor's offices), the principal church (*parroquia* in our case, since the bishop was in Durango and the cathedral was there), and the *cabildo*, the city hall, which is almost invariably directly opposite the church in Mexican cities. Examples in Mexico of cities planned in this manner would include Guadalajara, Mexico City, and Oaxaca. Some of these rules are in evidence in Santa Fe.

The earliest map we have of Santa Fe was drafted by Joseph de Urrutia in 1766. This map is truly a treasure. Urrutia did not include any streets in his map but did indicate the *"caminos"* heading to locations out of Santa Fe. Streets can be inferred from the plaza—one street to the north and one to the south. The plaza, if we excise that one building to the southeast of the palace in the Urrutia map, is very large, probably because Santa Fe was the capital of the province. But perhaps because the plaza was eventually perceived as being overly large, building began in the eastern portion, diminishing its size to what we see today.

Although it was proclaimed La Villa Real de Santa Fé de San Francisco, the city, in fact, did not amount to much. In its early years, about one thousand people lived in the vicinity of Santa Fe. By 1776 the city had grown to twenty-three hundred residents, but these residents were mostly farmers living on their farmsteads up and down the Río de Santa Fe. In the census of 1790, just one merchant was listed for the city. Zebulon Pike, in 1807, wrote that Santa Fe was three streets wide and stretched along the river for about one mile.

Farming, which was mostly subsistence farming in Santa Fe, required water for the crops. This water for irrigation was distributed by means of acequias, two of which are indicated on the Urrutia map. We know that once streets and plazas are laid down, they remain in place; they rarely move to new locations. If this is true for streets, it is doubly true for acequias. One of those narrow lines on Urrutia's map is still with us as the Acequia Madre, the "mother ditch." This six-mile-long acequia will be detailed below. The second acequia shown on the map, the Acequia de la Muralla (wall), is long gone.

The roads persist as well. To the northwest went the Camino de la Cañada. This reference is to the villa of Santa Cruz de la Cañada, near today's Española. To the southwest ran the Camino del Álamo, the Camino Real as it left for El Álamo, Santo Domingo, and Mexico City. The Camino de Galisteo ran south to the Galisteo basin. Two caminos are shown heading to Pecos; that would have been the pueblo at Pecos. The western one is today's Old Santa Fe Trail, while the eastern branch follows García Street. Thus, using the persistence of the old caminos and acequias, we find that a number of places on Urrutia's map can be located precisely today.

Santa Fe's very street pattern is one of its charms. You'll need a good city map, which you can buy almost anywhere. The city is an important tourist destination with no real "downtime." The town has a number of parking lots, but you might consider the one on the south side of the river behind San Miguel Chapel. It's an easy walk to the plaza from here, and parking is free. Another advantage to parking here is that the state maintains a tourist information center next to the chapel, which means you can stop there on your way to the plaza. A tourist information center is on the west side of the plaza.

A tour of Camino Real sites should begin at the plaza. Points of interest are described below—some you can walk to; others you'll need to drive to in your car.

Acequias

Acequias are simply irrigation ditches. The Spanish brought this technology with them when they came to settle New Mexico in 1598; the technology is likely Roman in origin and Arabic in name. One of the first tasks taken up in San Juan Pueblo shortly after Oñate arrived there was the construction of an acequia. It is easy to dismiss the importance and significance of these modest channels, but in northern New Mexico they can be very important. In many communities, the acequia association, the people entrusted with maintaining the acequia, forms an important element for Hispanic culture and its preservation.

The placement of this discussion here in the section on Santa Fe is no accident. One of the acequias shown on Urrutia's 1766 map is still functioning and winds its way some seven miles through Santa Fe neighborhoods. Called the Acequia Madre (mother ditch), it serves twenty-two households and is allowed sixty-six acre-feet of water from the Río Santa Fe to irrigate eighteen acres. Instead of fields of corn and beans, the water now nourishes lawns, fruit trees, and one pasture.

Acequia technology is not advanced. First a stream is needed that provides sufficient water during the growing season—in northern New Mexico, May through October. A small diversion dam, *presa* in Spanish, is built to divert the water from the stream into the acequia. The acequia would follow the contours of the land with a gentle descent planned to keep the water moving by gravity. Along its route smaller laterals, *sangrias* in Spanish (bloodletting), could be opened to allow individual farmers to irrigate their fields.

Today these acequia systems are governed by an acequia association. The *mayordomo* heads the association and supervises its operation with the help of three or four commissioners (*comisionados*). These association officers are elected by the water rights holders (*parciantes*). An assessment is made each year to maintain and repair the acequia with either labor or cash payments due from the parciantes.

Acequia systems are still found throughout northern New Mexico. One judge, in finding for an acequia association in a water dispute with a public utility, wrote that he believed "the preservation of these water rights is important to the vitality of a culture over three centuries old." South of La Bajada, most small acequia systems have been absorbed into large irrigation projects. But north of La Bajada, as here in Santa Fe, the acequias are thriving and with them the Hispanic culture.

SANTA FE

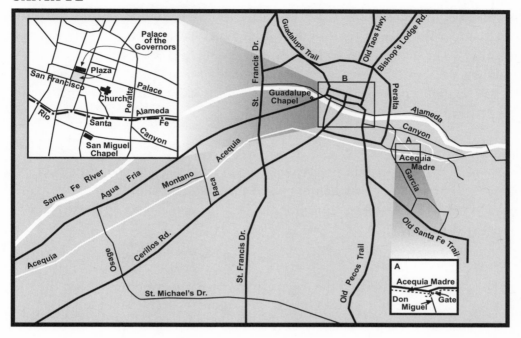

THE PLAZA AREA

The Santa Fe Plaza

The plaza is designated a registered National Historic Landmark. The bronze plaque for this designation is just inside the entrance to the Palace of the Governors. The plaza today is about half as large as originally planned. The block to the east, toward the cathedral, was most likely intended to be part of the plaza.

Palace of the Governors

On this site, some sort of building was constructed beginning in 1610, when the capital was moved here from San Juan Pueblo. It probably did not survive the Pueblo Revolt of 1680 and subsequent occupation by the victorious Indians. When de Vargas reconquered Santa Fe in 1693, the palace was constructed from scratch. Urrutia's map shows the palace occupying only the front portion of the site. Actually, the building should be named the Palacio de Gobierno, or "Palace of Government," not "Governors." But Urrutia himself labeled it "House of the Governor."

Today the palace is part of the Museum of New Mexico and houses many exhibits. The museum is continually attempting to piece together the history of the palace, each of its excavations answering some questions and posing others. The definitive story of this magnificent building will come sometime in the future.

Military Chapel Site
Opposite the Palace of the Governors, on San Francisco Street, is the site of the military chapel built there before 1766. A plaque on the building approximates the location. The chapel is shown on the Urrutia map as the Capilla de Nuestra Señora de la Luz.

St. Francis Cathedral
The cathedral was built in the American territorial period but sits on the site of the parroquia, the parish church. The adobe church that stood here was probably the third on this site when it was demolished to make way for the present cathedral. Actually, part of the earlier adobe church is incorporated into the present one. This location would have been at the eastern end of the original plaza.

The downtown area gives one a sense of Old Mexico. Narrow streets, many of which are curvilinear, add to the appeal. One block south of the plaza lies Water Street. Although Urrutia's map does not indicate an acequia here, a later map of 1846–47 by J. F. Gilmore clearly shows an acequia; hence the name "water." The Santa Fe Trail came into the plaza at the southeast corner, passing by La Fonda on its way. La Fonda is a more recent construction, but an earlier hotel was on this site, which marked the end of the famous trail that helped to shape this city and the history of the Southwest. Traders from north and east of Santa Fe began their contacts in 1821 and for the next twenty-five years brought increasing prosperity to the city and province.

Many Santa Fe traders did not stop in the city but continued south on the Camino Real, or Chihuahua Trail, as it was called by then. This commerce between American and Mexican traders freed New Mexico from economic dependence on Chihuahua and led to improving economic conditions in New Mexico. Note the "End of the Trail" Daughters of the American Revolution marker at the southeast corner of the plaza. This is the last of over 170 markers the DAR placed along the Santa Fe Trail.

Coronado Murals

Two murals showing explorer Francisco Vásquez de Coronado and Pueblo Indians in 1540 are found in the lobby of the U.S. Post Office on Federal Place two blocks north of the plaza.

BEYOND THE PLAZA AREA

San Miguel Chapel

This chapel is south of the Río Santa Fe on Old Santa Fe Trail. It was built to serve the residents of the Analco barrio, which surrounds the chapel. The marker in front of the chapel claims that it served the Tlascalan Indians who had come north with the Spaniards. Certainly the Tlascalans (a nation south and east of Mexico City that had helped Cortés conquer the Aztecs and thus was given preferential treatment by the Spaniards) had moved north with the Spanish. Mention is made of their help in Zacatecas and Sombrerete in pacifying those areas, but it is not known whether they came to Santa Fe in any numbers. The legend on the Urrutia map says that Analco was the barrio inhabited by the Tlascaltecas who had come with the conquerors.

Regardless of whom the chapel served, it is worth a visit. It had to be rebuilt after the Pueblo Revolt of 1680 and has been modified and strengthened many times since.

The Acequia Madre

To visit the acequia and its details, drive up Canyon (on the south side of the river) or Alameda (on the north side) and find Msgr. Patrick Smith Park, which is on Alameda. Park your car here and walk the short distance up Alameda to the bridge across the Río Santa Fe. On the north side of the bridge, you can see the headgate to the *acequia madre*, the mother ditch. You may have to climb down the bank to get a good look at it. This ditch is the southern one shown on the Urrutia map.

Every Wednesday during the growing season, water is sent down the acequia. It runs about six miles from this point to the last diversion, behind Agua Fría School. Return to your car, drive up Alameda, cross the bridge, and turn down Canyon. In a few blocks, you come to Acequia Madre Street, which is one way, so you have to detour to get to it. Continue on Canyon to the stop sign, turn left one block, and turn left again on Acequia Madre. Continue on Acequia Madre to Camino Don Miguel and park in the vicinity. Here you can find one of

The acequia madre, mother ditch, at its intersection with Canyon Road in Santa Fe. The photographer is T. Harmon Parkhurst. Courtesy Palace of the Governors, Neg. No.: 11047.

the diversions from the acequia. You'll see a gate that can be lowered into the acequia to raise the water level so that the water runs into a pair of sangrías, one on each side, which in turn carry the water to lawns and orchards of nearby homes. Several other such gates and associated sangrías can be seen farther down the acequia madre.

If you wish to pursue the acequia until it ends, you continue west on Acequia Madre street until it meets García Street. At this junction (you can locate this very point on the Urrutia map), take the street to your left front, Tenorio, which will take you to Old Santa Fe Trail, where you should turn right. Just before the signal light at Vargas, you will pass over the acequia. From here it goes to the south end of the railroad yard, and you can pick it up again at Guadalupe Street and Cerrillos Road. Continue west on Cerrillos and the acequia will be to your right. Drive to Baca and turn right; go to Potencia and turn left. Potencia becomes Montaño, which lies adjacent to the acequia. Continue on Montaño until it ends, turn right, and go to Agua Fría. Continue west on Agua Fría to Henry Lynch (just before Agua Fría School) and turn left onto Henry Lynch. In a long block, you pass over the now-diminished acequia, near its end.

SAN JUAN PUEBLO

Many think of Santa Fe as the northern terminus of the Camino Real, whereas in fact, Oñate's first capital, San Juan Pueblo, was some thirty miles north of Santa Fe in the area now called the Española valley. And if we include other public roads in use during colonial times, we can see that the camino extended as far as Taos. The sections north of Santa Fe are very appealing, with natural beauty combining with an overlay of Spanish and Indian landscapes.

Leave Santa Fe on US 285 heading north toward Española. As you ascend the hill (the national cemetery will be on your right), the camino, at least after 1610, parallels the highway on the left. Descend the hill, passing by the Santa Fe Opera and heading toward the pueblo of Tesuque, which will be to your left. The non-Indian community of Tesuque is to the east up the valley of the Río Tesuque. When Bishop Tamarón visited Tesuque in 1760, it held 31 families with 232 inhabitants. At the time, Tesuque was a *visita* of Santa Fe; that is, it had no resident priest but relied on "visits" of the Santa Fe priest.

As you continue north on US 84/285, the highway follows the camino. At Pojoaque, a Tewa pueblo at the time of Tamarón's visit, the road to Los Alamos (NM 502) goes west. If you turn here to visit Los Alamos, you pass by San Ildefonso Pueblo just before crossing the Rio Grande. This is another Tewa-speaking community found directly on the earliest (1598–1610) Camino Real. The camino split here at that time, with one branch crossing the Rio Grande, the other circling east and then heading north to San Juan Pueblo.

Continuing north from Pojoaque, you will pass the Arroyo Seco area, and a few miles farther, at a stoplight, turn right on NM 106. This road crosses the Río Santa Cruz in a few miles and ends at a stoplight. The prescribed route here will direct you left and on toward San Juan Pueblo and Taos. Returning from Taos later, you will visit Chimayó, which is just a few miles up the valley, and then return to this point.

Turn left at the light—the highway is now NM 76/106—and go about one mile, then turn right toward the Santa Cruz church on a road called South McCurdy. Shortly after turning onto McCurdy, you arrive at the church and small plaza.

Santa Cruz de la Cañada

Santa Cruz de la Cañada was one of four villas designated in the province of New Mexico. (Santa Fe, El Paso del Norte, and Albuquerque were the other three.) When de Vargas reoccupied northern New Mexico in 1693, he asked for

Santa Fe to Taos

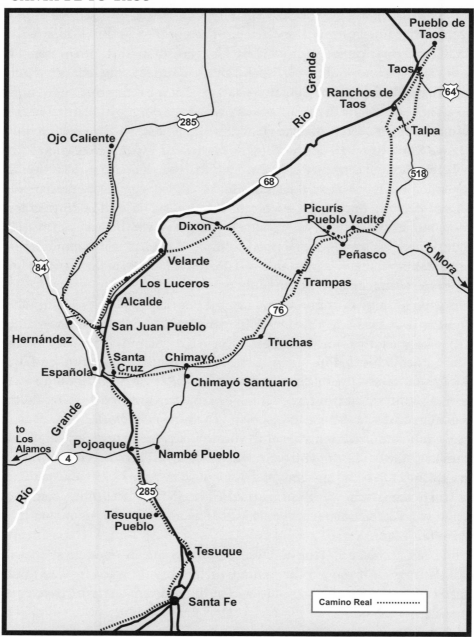

Church in Santa Cruz, one of the state's oldest. Photo by author.

additional settlers from the viceroy in Mexico City. In response to his request, 67 families of 235 persons came up the Camino Real, reaching Santa Fe in June 1693. After a pause of ten months in the capital, most of this group came on to Santa Cruz. Bishop Tamarón noted at the time of his visit in 1760 that there were 241 families in Santa Cruz, with 1,515 individuals. He stated that there was "no semblance of a town," with residents living over a wide area. Such dispersal was the rule in each of the villas, with most residents choosing to live near their farms, where they could keep a close eye on their crops and animals.

The church, begun in about 1733, is one of the state's oldest. Looking at the community today, one finds it hard to imagine it was ever a villa, since villas were to have followed a plan where streets and blocks were laid out in a grid pattern. The Laws of the Indies had prescribed this system for towns in the New World. And as Tamarón noted, hardly anyone lived here in 1760. One has to wonder if there had ever been a plan.

McCurdy is the Camino Real here, so follow it north toward San Juan Pueblo. The road winds through the valley and after a few stop signs arrives at a T. If you direct your eyes straight ahead across the road here, you can see a faint trace that is the camino going toward San Juan Pueblo. Turn left here, at

SAN JUAN PUEBLO AND SAN GABRIEL

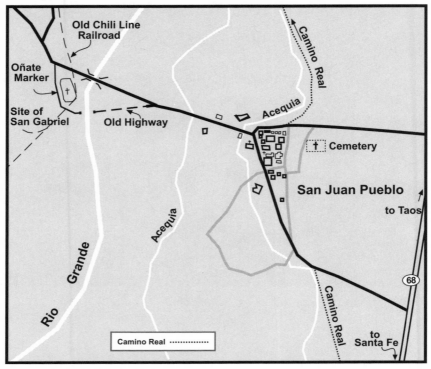

NM 291, and continue to the stop sign, where you find the principal north-south road, NM 68, which leads to Taos.

Turn right on NM 68 and drive north, passing a large Indian casino, Ohkay, on your right. Just past the casino (one-half mile) is a turn to the left, west, clearly marked for the San Juan Pueblo. The pueblo's name will likely change to Ohkay Owingeh, the Indian name, in the future. Take this road and follow it to a point just before it bends to the right (see map). The road to your left is the camino as it came from Santa Cruz. You can drive south on this road, and at a point opposite the casino, you can detect a faint road to your left heading south toward Santa Cruz and McCurdy Road. This was the camino in colonial times.

Ohkay Oweenge

San Juan Pueblo, or Ohkay Owingeh, as the Indians called it, was chosen by Juan de Oñate to be his capital. Oñate arrived here with his vanguard on July 10, 1598. At first Oñate called it San Juan de Bautista but later San Juan de los Caballeros,

*Marker at San Gabriel commemorating Juan de Oñate and
the establishment of the first capital. Photo by author.*

in honor of the *caballeros*, or gentlemen, who had so graciously welcomed and
assisted him.

Scholars debate which was Oñate's first or second choice for a site for the
capital. It was moved across the Rio Grande soon after the caravan arrived, into
the site of a smaller pueblo called Yunge. The Indians resident at Yunge moved
back across the river to Ohkay.

It is known that in August 1598, one month after arriving in this area, the
Spaniards (with fifteen hundred Indians doing the work) began construction of
an acequia. In the same month, a crudely built church was constructed. Oñate
named this new community on the west side of the Rio Grande San Gabriel del
Yunge Oweenge.

The pueblo of San Juan today is a somnolent village. As you pass through,
you will see two churches, one on each side of the road, both built in the late nineteenth century. Behind the church on your right (east) is the principal plaza. Just
past the churches, you will arrive at a stop sign, where you should turn left on
NM 74. Before you cross the Rio Grande on the "new bridge," you can see the old
road and bridge to your left. Cross over the river and immediately turn left over a

cattle guard, which places you on the old road. Continue down this road, looking for a cross on a mound to your left. Park on the road near an opening in the fence.

San Gabriel

This mound is part of the old Yunge pueblo. If you look to the southwest, you can see a small orchard in the distance. The orchard is found in the old Spanish town of San Gabriel. Excavations here in the 1960s located the pueblo, the Spanish dwellings, and the footings for the church. Unfortunately, all those locations are on private land and not open to the public. The San Juan tribe hopes to begin a program in which visitors can be escorted from a proposed visitor center to the San Gabriel site. For now, all you can do is view the site from the mound and marker honoring Oñate's achievements.

OJO CALIENTE

Returning to your car, you can, if you wish, detour here (it will be thirty-four miles round-trip) to visit an old Spanish community called Ojo Caliente. To do this, continue west on NM 74 until you meet US 285, where you drive north to Ojo Caliente (hot spring). Governor Juan Bautista de Anza passed through Ojo Caliente in August 1779, on his way north on a punitive mission against the Comanches. He called it "a deserted pueblo at the end of the Camino Real," since it was abandoned at the time as a result of Indian hostilities. Anza wanted villages such as Ojo Caliente to become fortified plazas so that the Spaniards could protect themselves against Indian attacks.

Anza's was not a popular policy, but his plans must have been adopted in Ojo Caliente, for when Zebulon Pike, after his capture in southern Colorado by Spanish troops in 1807, was brought south through Ojo Caliente, he described the community in a manner that clearly indicates it was built as a defensive town, or fortified plaza. Pike described Ojo Caliente as "a square enclosure of mud walls, the houses forming the wall." He wrote that the residents were "civilized Indians," which we know as *genízaros*. Indian children traded for at the several fairs in New Mexico (Taos and Pecos) were assigned to Spanish families who were charged with their upbringing, including making Christians of them. These were the civilized Indians noted by Pike.

Today the hot springs are still is use, part of a modest resort surrounding the springs. There is no sign of the fortified plaza today, but two churches are where the plaza would have been. The smaller, and older, of the two has a marker nearby that says it is La Santa Cruz Church, built after 1793. The marker goes

Genízaros

One group of New Mexicans that deserves recognition is the genízaros. Many eighteenth-century communities were settled by these important folk. The name *genízaro* is a peculiar one and not found in modern dictionaries. In the fifteenth-century expansion of the Ottoman Empire into the Balkans, children were captured, separated from their families, and trained as soldiers. The English word for such soldiers is *janissary*. They were used particularly on the frontiers of Turkey and were considered loyal guards and soldiers.

The New Mexican genízaros were a result of the introduction of Indian children, bartered for at the trade fairs at Taos and Pecos pueblos. Those two pueblos became centers of commerce between Spanish and Indian. Children captured by one tribe would later be bartered for and assigned to a Spanish family, which would be charged with raising the child as a good Christian. The genízaros formed their own communities in established New Mexican towns but soon were seeking land on which to farm and form families.

In the mid-eighteenth century, the Spanish population had claim on most irrigable land between Albuquerque and Santa Cruz, so the genízaros were assigned land on the edge of the province, on the frontiers. Tomé and Belen in the south were begun by genízaros, and Abiquiu and Ojo Caliente were similar northern genízaro communities.

Those citizen-soldiers successfully defended the province's frontier against Indian attacks. Today few residents of genízaro towns recognize the important role their ancestors played in early New Mexico history.

on to say the church was licensed in 1812. It probably was here when Pike passed through in 1807, although he did not mention a church. Return to US 285 and turn south toward San Juan Pueblo. When Pike was taken down this valley in 1807, he noted several small villages, all of which had round mud towers "to defend the inhabitants from the intrusions of savages." These round mud towers we know as *torreones*. You will see the remains of a torreon in Taos.

Return to San Juan Pueblo by way of NM 74. Just a few hundred yards past the road that leads back into the pueblo (this is the road you utilized earlier) is a road to your left. Take this road, for it is almost directly on the camino and passes through several very attractive areas on its way to Velarde, at the mouth of the Rio Grande canyon.

DIXON AND EMBUDO PASS

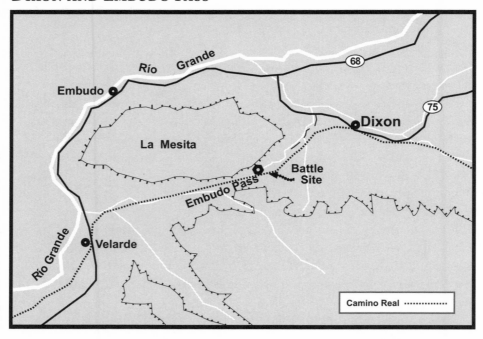

For the first two miles, you are in the land grant of San Juan Pueblo, grant-ed to the inhabitants in 1689. The first community you come to is a Hispanic one called Alcalde. The camino along this route follows a pattern you'll see later as you drive south from Santa Fe. The road occupies that first terrace above the floodplain of the Rio Grande. The acequia, or irrigation ditch, occupies almost exactly the same path. The camino, by being slightly above the floodplain, was dry and firm for travel by carts. The floodplain, often wet from overflow during times of floods, was where the farmlands were.

Continuing north from Alcalde, you will pass Villita and Los Luceros. At Villita look for a paved road on the right that will take you up out of the valley to rejoin NM 68. The Oñate Center is here on the east side of NM 68, just north of mile marker 8. A very nice equestrian statue of don Juan de Oñate sits between the highway and the center. Fame, of sorts, was bestowed on this statue a few years ago when vandals cut off one of Oñate's feet to remind everyone of crimes against the Acoma Indians, supposedly at Oñate's behest. After visiting the Oñate Center, you can either continue north on NM 68 or, better, turn back west to rejoin the camino as it heads toward Los Luceros and Velarde.

At Velarde the camino left the river because the canyon was too hazardous for carts. After meeting NM 68 at Velarde (at or near a gas station), continue on NM 68 to the north end of the community and turn right (east) on County Road 1073. Drive to the end of this road (at a sand-and-gravel quarry) and stop. The camino continued up this canyon before turning northeast to pass through Embudo Pass. We'll pick up the camino at the north end of that pass.

Return to NM 68 and turn right. The road enters the canyon and follows the river very closely here, passing by Embudo Station (on the west side of the river), which was a stop on the long-gone Chili narrow-gauge railway. At La Junta (the junction) the road crosses Embudo Creek, and soon thereafter you come to the junction with NM 75 for Dixon. Turn right here and drive 1.1 miles to a point where a creek bed lies almost across the road. Turn right here on a dirt road and drive about 0.3 mile and stop. Ahead is Embudo Pass, which was the scene of a battle between forces of the U.S. Army and New Mexican rebels on January 29, 1847. The rebels lost the battle and retreated north to Taos.

The camino came through this pass and turned east, passing through present-day Dixon (then called Embudo). It continued up the creek and turned up Cañada de Ojo Sarco, finally arriving at the community of Trampas. Today you can't drive this route through the canyon, so instead return to NM 68 and follow the road north toward Taos. Although the camino did not use this route, pack trains, *atajos*, could and did use it. In winter, because of snow in the higher elevations, the river route would have been the only connection with the Taos communities.

Drive north on NM 68 following the river, which will be on your left until you reach Pilar. At Pilar the pack train route continued up the Rio Grande for a few miles before ascending to the Taos terrace. From there the trail headed straight for Taos and Taos Pueblo. You will remain on NM 68 and will see several pullouts from which you can view the Rio Grande gorge. It is easy to understand why the gorge was a major barrier to east-west traffic.

Taos Valley

Taos Pueblo is the northernmost pueblo in New Mexico and was probably established in about AD 1350. The Taos Indians are Tiwa speakers, closely related to those Indians in Sandia and Isleta pueblos today. The first European to visit the Taos area was one of Coronado's captains, Hernando de Alvarado, who entered the valley in 1540.

Soon after his *entrada* into New Mexico in 1598 and the establishment of the capital at San Juan Pueblo, Oñate came north to Taos, complaining at the time of

Taos area

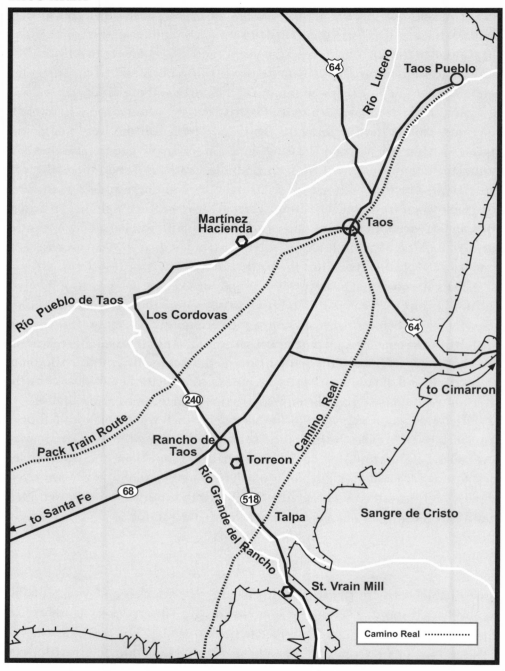

six leagues (one league is about four miles) of bad road between Picurís Pueblo and Taos (he followed the high road, the one you will use to return to Santa Fe). In August 1598, Padre Francisco de Zamora was placed in charge of both Taos and Picurís pueblos. A few Spanish settlers followed soon thereafter. At the time of the Pueblo Revolt in 1680, seventy settlers and two priests were killed here, so we can infer that the Spanish intrusion, in terms of numbers, had been modest.

After the de Vargas reconquest, a few land grants were made to Spaniards in the Taos valley. The first, made in 1716 to Antonio Martínez, included present-day Los Ranchos de Taos. When Bishop Tamarón visited Taos Pueblo in 1760, he reported 159 Indian families with 505 persons and 36 families of "citizens" (Spaniards) with 160 persons. The number of Spaniards increased to about three hundred by 1776, most of them living in the Ranchos de Taos area. The Spanish settlers from the vicinity of Taos Pueblo moved to the present Taos area by the late eighteenth century.

The Taos valley was always to be a frontier area. If other communities had some contact with Plains Indians, the Taos (and Pecos) Pueblo had more. Taos was made the site of an annual trade fair as early as 1723, when Plains Indians brought their buffalo hides and captured Indians to exchange for Spanish goods. Utes, Navajos, Apaches, and Comanches came to know the Taos area only too well. In 1760 Tamarón reported on an attack on Taos by three thousand Comanche warriors. As you will see later, the Comanches continued their attacks into the nineteenth century, striking as far south as Durango, Mexico.

Several locations in the valley are camino related. After visiting all of them, you will take the route south and return to Ranchos, then head southeast toward Trampas and Chimayó.

Ranchos de Taos

The first community you come to as you near Taos on NM 68 is Ranchos de Taos. The center of attention in Ranchos is its church, San Francisco de Asís. Built in 1810, this church is said to be the most-photographed building in New Mexico. You will see it to your right just after you cross the stream on NM 68. The first view you have of the church is the rear, so you must park and walk around to admire it and its small plaza. The Ranchos community extended far up the modest stream to the south of the plaza.

Martínez Hacienda

Leaving Ranchos, you should cross over NM 68 and head north on NM 240. This route will take you by the old Martínez hacienda and eventually to Taos,

Taos

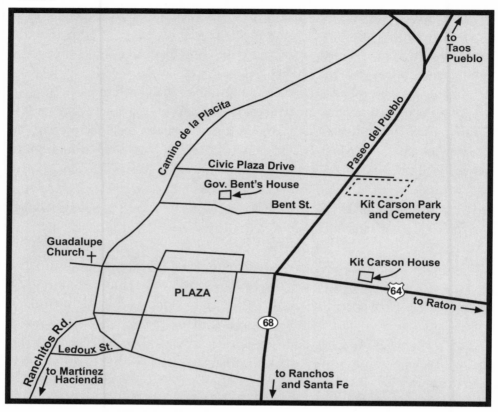

essentially following the pack train route. When you reach the hacienda, be sure to stop and visit it. The hacienda was built in 1804 by the Martínez family. One member was Padre José Antónío Martínez, the implacable foe of Bishop Lamy. Lamy, the first bishop of New Mexico, excommunicated Martínez without, it seems, ill effect—Martínez's flock continued to follow his leadership. It was Martínez who married Kit Carson and Josefa Jaramillo.

Taos

From the hacienda, continue northeast to the center of Taos. This town likely dates from the 1790s. Settlers who had been living closer to the pueblo north of here moved to this Taos site during that period. The present plaza is only one of several plazas found in the town at an earlier date. The large parking lot to the north of the plaza is the location of one of the earlier plazas.

The plaza is one block west of NM 68 (see map). Today the plaza is filled with commercial shops, many of them catering to the extensive tourist trade in the city. It certainly has the appearance of a fortified plaza. Buildings connect, and narrow openings can be found at the corners of the plaza. The church is actually one block from here, but on another plaza.

Two other points of interest in Taos, although not Camino Real oriented, are worth a visit. First, the house of Kit Carson, who lived in Taos and for several years served as government agent for the Utes and Jicarilla Apaches, is now a museum and imparts a feel of the times when Carson lived here. The house stands just east of the plaza on US 64. Second, the house that was occupied by Governor Charles Bent at the time of the revolt is on Bent Street, just north of the plaza. Bent was assassinated here in January 1847. A hole punched through a wall is supposed to have been cut at the time to allow Bent's family to escape.

Taos Pueblo

Leave Taos on NM 68, heading north until you reach a Y. In the center of the Y, you will see an official New Mexico Historic Marker, Taos Pueblo. Take the right fork and go two miles to the pueblo, where you will pay an entrance fee for a visit.

Taos Pueblo is the archetype for what we think pueblos should be. It is a spectacular adobe pueblo divided into two parts by a rushing creek. In January 1847, New Mexican rebels had fought several battles with approaching U.S. Army troops. One skirmish took place at Santa Cruz, another at Embudo Pass. Here in the Taos valley the conflict came to a bitter end. Rebels killed Governor Charles Bent (one of the Bent brothers of Bent's Fort fame) and others. They then took refuge in the church at Taos Pueblo, where the American army captured them after a bloody battle on February 3 and 4, 1847. A subsequent trial brought a sentence of death for several of them. Just before entering the plaza, on your left, you can still see the ruins of the church that was the last refuge for the rebels before it was battered down by Colonel Sterling Price's artillery.

After visiting the pueblo, return to Taos and continue south to NM 518, which you reach just before entering Ranchos de Taos. This is what Governor de Anza said as he left Taos for Santa Fe: "At half-past seven, we continued our march along the Camino Real to Santa Fe." You will turn left on NM 518, and at 0.7 mile, you can see the base of a torreon (tower) on the right. It's hard to spot because it's back from the road one hundred yards but worth seeking out. Many communities had such torreons in colonial times as a way of spotting approaching Indians and protecting their residents.

At about 0.8 mile beyond the torreon, the camino crosses the highway,

Base of a torreon near Ranchos de Taos. Torreones would
have been a common feature in many colonial communities.
Photo by author.

headed for Taos. The route is visible on the north side of NM 518, embedded in a narrow rock-lined lane. Continue on NM 518, and just after passing into the Carson National Forest at 3.5 miles from NM 68, you will find the approximate location of Ceran St. Vrain's gristmill.

Ceran St. Vrain, Charles Bent, and William Bent were important figures in trade along the Santa Fe Trail. It was they who established Bent's Fort on the Arkansas River in the 1830s as a trading post. Charles Bent was the first territorial governor of New Mexico but was murdered in Taos by the rebels in 1847. St. Vrain began his gristmill here in 1850 to supply flour for the nearby fort of Cantonment Burgwin. In 1855 he moved to Mora, where he built another mill (to supply Fort Union this time). He died there in 1870.

Just past the St. Vrain mill site on your right, you will see an entrance to the Southern Methodist University research site on the grounds where Cantonment Burgwin was situated. If the gate is open, you can enter and visit the restored cantonment. As a result of the uprising in Taos, the U.S. Army thought they needed a military presence in the Taos area. In 1852 construction began on

Cantonment Burgwin, named after Captain John Burgwin, who had died in Taos during the revolt. The structure lasted until 1860, when the troops were reassigned to other posts.

Continue south on NM 518 up a narrowing canyon. The camino is to your right here, some three miles over the ridge. Finally, you will reach the junction of NM 518 and NM 75. Turn right at this junction on NM 75 heading to Vadito. Vadito is on the Río Pueblo, which continues to Picurís Pueblo. The camino passed through Vadito and turned north there up Telegraph Canyon. The camino ascended the canyon, taking a right branch, Osha Canyon, to summit the Picurís Mountains before descending Arroyo Miranda into Ranchos de Taos. This stretch of the road, of course, could not be used in winter because of snow.

From Vadito, continue through Peñasco, then turn left on NM 76 for Trampas. On this portion of NM 76, you are close to the route of the camino. As you enter the Trampas area, note the *canoa* taking water over an arroyo. This canoa may very well be the only remaining example in New Mexico of the old technique of hollowing out a log to carry water.

After leaving Trampas, you will ascend a modest hill before dropping once again, this time into the Cañada de Ojo Sarco. The camino ascended this *cañada* after leaving Dixon, which you visited earlier. From Ojo Sarco, continue south to Truchas (Truchas had momentary fame as the site of the filming of *The Milagro Beanfield War*). Continue to Chimayó, which lies at the head of the Santa Cruz valley.

Chimayó

Chimayó is noted for its weavings, fine examples of which can be viewed and purchased at numerous locations in the vicinity. You can park near a prominent store in Chimayó, called Ortega's, then take an easy walk of a block to the historic plaza.

Earlier, mention was made of the fortified plaza noted by Zebulon Pike at Ojo Caliente. That one has disappeared, but the plaza here at Chimayó remains a fine example of a fortified plaza. From Ortega's, walk a few hundred feet to the south, where a sign will point you to the small museum, and there you will find the plaza. You can stroll through the plaza and get a sense of its purpose. Buildings are attached, and even today there are only a few openings into the plaza area. In colonial times, there were probably only two openings, which would have had gates that could be closed at night or in times of peril. More recently, buildings have intruded into the plaza area.

A popular tourist site stands nearby at the Santuario de Chimayó, where a small family chapel attracts thousands of pilgrims at Easter time. The santuario is but a mile or so south of the plaza. Continue down the pleasant Santa Cruz valley on NM 76 to Santa Cruz de la Cañada, where you can rejoin US 285 for the return to Santa Fe.

Leave Santa Fe by way of Agua Fría Street, which is adjacent to the Guadalupe Chapel. This route will take you south on the Camino Real, the route that Urrutia called Camino del Álamo on his map. The camino here runs along the ridge between the arroyo of the Río Santa Fe and that of the Arroyo de los Chamisos to the south.

Look for the Agua Fría church on your left adjacent to the street. The gate to the church says San Isidro Church, 1835. San Isidro is the patron saint of farmers, so Agua Fría was a farming community until the recent past, when it became a bedroom community for Santa Fe. An Indian pueblo stood here before the Spanish arrived, but it was burned. An early name for this area was Quemado, Spanish for "burned." Agua Fría is mentioned by travelers but only in passing, since it was too near Santa Fe to be utilized as a *paraje*, or rest stop.

Continuing southwest on Agua Fría, you will need to make a sharp left (you can see where the camino lies straight ahead as you turn). Next you will come to a stoplight at Airport Road. Turn right here and continue toward the airport. At 1.1 miles, you come to a major intersection with NM 599, the new bypass that skirts Santa Fe on the way north to the Española valley and Taos. It is about here where the camino splits, with one branch going straight ahead to Cieneguilla and La Bajada mesa and the other bending left toward El Álamo, Golondrinas, and La Ciénega. You will visit these last sites later, so stay the course and continue on Airport Road.

Cross NM 599 and continue past the turn to the airport. You will now be on Santa Fe County Road 56. Pass over the small Río Santa Fe, and at two miles from NM 599, you will find a sign for the Santa Fe Horse Park. Do not take this road but continue 1.3 miles past the first sign and you will arrive at a second sign for the horse park. The road to your right is marked Santa Fe County Road 56C.

You have a choice here. The road to your right follows the Camino Real that was used by horses and probably mule trains, atajos. It climbs up onto La Bajada mesa and goes south to a dramatic drop of some six hundred feet. Few wagons could have used this route, but anyone on horse would have preferred it because it was shorter and easier for them. This road, interestingly enough, became the road of old Route 66. The latter highway (before 1936) came through Santa Fe and went south on La Bajada mesa before going on to Albuquerque.

SANTA FE TO LA BAJADA

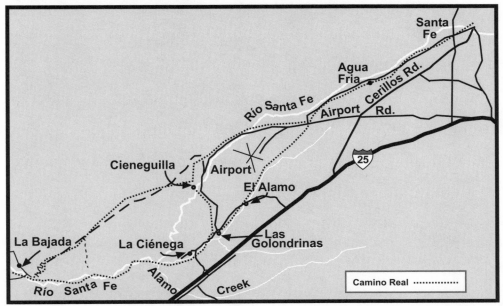

The road is gravel and dirt and is satisfactory for cars if there have been no recent rains and one uses caution. This side trip is highly recommended, as you will see elements of the camino not visible elsewhere.

Take the road and it will gently rise up onto the mesa. You will be passing through land controlled by the Bureau of Land Management and National Forest Service. When you get on the top of the mesa, note the power line to your right and keep in mind that the camino (and Route 66) parallels the line. You will pass through several cattle gates on your way south. At about seven miles from where you left the pavement, you can see a water tank and windmill to your left. Take the dirt road that leads toward them. Continue past them, pass under another set of power lines, and you will arrive at the lip of the Cañon del Río Santa Fe.

You can park here and see the amphitheater below you with the canyon beyond. An Indian pueblo, Tsinat, was once in this amphitheater, but it was not occupied in Spanish times. A decent trail leads down into the amphitheater and beyond into the canyon. If you look carefully, you can see the camino following the course of the river below. This would have been the major route for the wagon trains. It was somewhat challenging because at times the river would

Scene in the canyon of the Santa Fe River. Gentle swales of the Camino Real are visible. Photo courtesy Pat Macklin.

have been high, and one would also have had to cross and recross the river many times as it meandered from side to side in its canyon.

Although most of the canyon, controlled by the Bureau of Land Management and the National Forest Service, is open to the public, the "ends" of the canyon are not on public lands, so one cannot enter from them.

Return to old Route 66 and continue toward the south. Finally, you reach the point where the camino (and Route 66) had to make a precipitous drop off the mesa. As Zebulon Pike left Santa Fe and came by this route on March 4, 1807, he wrote that he went three miles before ascending a hill and finally came "to a precipice, which we descended with great difficulty, from the obscurity of the night, to the small village." When you come to the end of the road, you are peering over the precipice about which Pike wrote. And the community you can see at the foot of the mesa is Pike's small village, now called La Bajada. You will stop there later in your trip.

This is one of the most engrossing places to view the old camino. There are actually two variants of the Camino Real that met at the entrance of Las Bocas,

From the edge of the mesa at La Bajada, one can see the older route of the Camino Real. Photo by author.

the Cañon del Río Santa Fe. The earlier one is visible to the right front just west and parallel to the paved road you see. This branch passed through the old Keres pueblo of La Bajada. The slightly later variant, developed after the demise of the pueblo, headed directly toward Las Bocas. You can see this trace if you look carefully to your left. If you have trouble discerning these routes, consult the accompanying map and photo. Today this panorama is unmatched along the route of the camino. You will visit both variants of the camino later on your trip.

Return to the paved road by the same route you came by. At the pavement, turn right and you will quickly pass over the Río Santa Fe. At about one

Camino Real Route Variant

The wagon and cart road up Las Bocas, or Cañada de Río Santa Fé, was always a problem. Even today, ascending the canyon requires one to cross and recross the river many times as it oscillates from side to side in the canyon. Climbing directly up La Bajada escarpment (six hundred feet vertical) was suitable for horses and mules but hardly for carts.

Sometime during the late colonial (or perhaps early Mexican) period, an alternate route was developed. From the south, this route left the established route just north of San Felipe Pueblo. It ascended the gentle hills and passed almost exactly where the Mormon Battalion marker is on Interstate 25. From there, this camino continued northeast, descending into the Galisteo basin.

What made this route preferable was that it ascended from the Río Galisteo just east of the terminus of La Bajada volcanic escarpment. The camino climbed a series of gravel benches before reaching La Bajada mesa, where it continued on flat ground to La Ciénega and joined the established route there.

The alternate route is called the Juana López to San Felipe camino. It was heavily used when the Santa Fe Trail traders extended their trips south to Chihuahua. Apparently this was the route used by General Kearny and his troops in 1847, when they left Santa Fe for California.

Improvements were made along this road in 1858 and 1859 by the U.S. Army. In 1858 the north ascent out of the Galisteo basin was improved, and in 1859 more improvements were made, this time by building a bridge on the southern ascent of the Galisteo. A small portion of this bridge is still in place.

To see portions of this route, continue east over the La Ciénega exit (Exit 271) on I-25 to the frontage road. Turn right onto the frontage road and continue south about one-half mile to a paved road to the left. Take this road, and after one hundred yards you will see a row of small juniper trees on the left (north) side. If you look carefully, you will note that these junipers are in a shallow swale of the camino.

mile after you rejoin the pavement, the road makes a sharp turn to the left and goes up a small hill. To the immediate right you can see a field with many mounds in it. This is the site of yet another old Indian pueblo. At Paseo de San Antonio, at the top of the hill, turn right and drive a few hundred yards and stop.

On your right, between you and the river, is the small mission chapel of San Antonio, which served the community of Cieneguilla. Most residents of

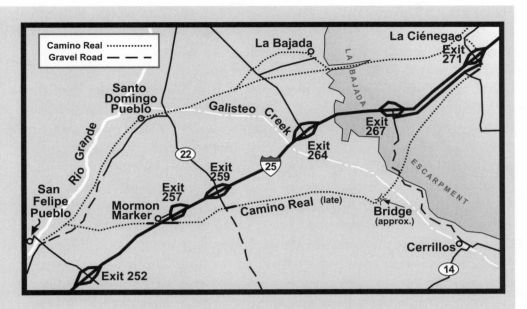

From here return to the frontage road and turn left. As you drive south, the camino parallels you on your left. Just past the rest area (not accessible from the frontage road), you come to another exit of I-25 (Exit 267). Go left here (it's Waldo Road) and follow the road until it begins to descend from the mesa. This descent certainly lies above the old camino.

Return to the interstate and go south. At the Budaghers exit (Exit 257), you should exit and follow signs to the frontage road going south to the Mormon Battalion marker. Pass the marker and stop at the very end of the old road near a small tree. Behind that tree are faint traces of the camino's swales. The swales on the east side of the interstate are more dramatic, but you must be going north on the interstate to see them. Stop directly opposite the Mormon Battalion marker and look to the right. Two clear swales are here, heading off to the northeast and the Galisteo basin.

Cieneguilla lived and farmed on the other side of the river. In 1782 nine families were living here.

From Cieneguilla it was not possible to continue down the Río Santa Fe because the canyon here was too narrow. Travelers would leave the river here and go over the hill to Las Golondrinas. To get to Las Golondrinas, return to the main road, turn right, and drive 1.3 miles to the picturesque valley of La Ciénega Creek.

LAS GOLONDRINAS

There were three named places in this valley. The oldest, La Ciénega, is to your right here, and you will visit it later. And you will certainly want to stop at Las Golondrinas, where the roads meet, and visit this living history museum. Included at Las Golondrinas are an eighteenth-century home and defensive tower, or torreon, and a multitude of summer activities offered by the museum. This is one site that should mot be missed. In 1780 Governor Juan Bautista de Anza passed through here, calling it the pueblo of Las Golondrinas. A marker commemorating the Anza visit is just inside the entrance to the museum.

After visiting Las Golondrinas, drive to your right, up the valley, to see the area called El Álamo. Recall that Urrutia's map of Santa Fe in 1766 shows the Camino del Álamo, the road to El Álamo. Bishop Tamarón stayed at El Álamo in 1760, mentioning the large house with an upper story. The first house on your right after you leave Las Golondrinas is probably a part of the house mentioned by Tamarón. As you drive along, you will pass two small arroyos, each with occasional water in them. The principal creek lies to your right. Most likely a series of farms lay along this route, in an area called El Álamo after the number of large cottonwood trees lining the watercourses.

At 1.7 miles from Las Golondrinas, the road will leave the arroyo and go to the east. At this point, Paseo del Angel intersects the highway. To the north of this intersection, one can still see slight swales where the camino continued up the arroyo toward Agua Fría and Santa Fe.

From this point, it is suggested that you turn around, return to Golondrinas, and continue down the valley to La Ciénega. This stretch of the road almost certainly lies directly above the camino. You will know when you reach La Ciénega because the road makes a turn to the left and crosses the creek. The camino continued down this valley to La Bajada and most likely stayed on the north side of the creek. There is a road on this side, but after about a mile, it is posted no trespassing. When La Ciénega Creek meets the Río Santa Fe in about two miles, it is easy to follow the camino as it meanders down the valley.

Cross over the creek and drive east to Interstate 25. At this point, you have the choice of following the older Camino Real or using directions below to locate a later variant of the camino. If you choose to remain on the older camino, join the interstate here and drive south to Exit 264.

CHAPTER TWO

La Bajada to Fra Cristóbal

LA BAJADA

Descend La Bajada on Interstate 25 and leave at the first exit (Exit 264), where a sign will say Cochiti Lake. Follow NM 16 for 3.8 miles to the intersection with a paved road from the right. This road will take you to the base of La Bajada. Two visible scars of the Camino Real are near this intersection. The older of the two, just north of (beyond) the intersection, is the one that connected the now-abandoned pueblo of La Bajada with the pueblo at Santo Domingo. If you park near the intersection, you can walk north a few yards and view this swale on the east (right).

A later route was established after the demise of La Bajada Pueblo, when travelers headed directly from the mouth (*boca*) of the canyon to Santo Domingo Pueblo. To view this route, you have to back track a few hundred yards and look for the gentle swales on the east, which point directly to the white rocks at Las Bocas. This spot is near the point where NM 16 jogs.

Turn right at the intersection and drive 1.1 miles paralleling the power lines on your right. Adjacent to the power lines, you can detect traces of old Route 66. At 1.1 miles, turn right and then immediately left onto a gravel road. You are now on top of old Route 66 going to La Bajada. As you approach the mesa, you will see a bridge across the Río Santa Fe, but before that bridge is a pair of dirt roads leading to your right. Take either one and follow it to a gate. You are now at Las

Las Bocas at La Bajada

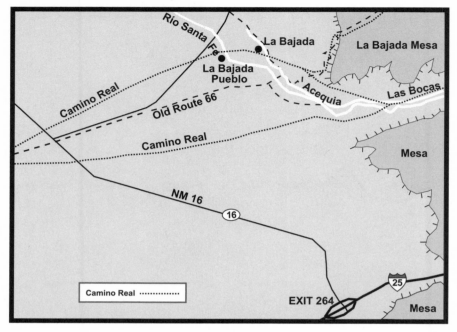

Bocas, the mouth of the Cañada de Santa Fé. From here you can walk to your right and find parts of the camino, the later route that you saw a few minutes ago on NM 16. You can also walk to the river's edge and look across to see the acequia, which still delivers water to the small community of La Bajada. Almost all of the cañada is in the public domain. If you look beyond the gate, you can see another gate a few hundred yards away—that stretch is the only section that is private. The camino went up this canyon, crossing the river many times as it swung from side to side. Travelers emerged near the community of La Ciénega, where the valley widens.

Return to old Route 66, turn right, cross over the bridge, and park near the base of the mesa. If you wish to walk up the old road, which you can clearly see here, it will take about forty-five minutes, with a vertical climb of about six hundred feet. The walk is well worth the effort. If you choose to climb, stay to your left because a fork about one-quarter of the way up leading off to the right is a later route built for Route 66. At the top, you will have a remarkable view of the camino's two paths and the small village. This is the same spot you were at earlier if you chose to drive on the mesa.

*Las Bocas, the mouth of the Santa Fe canyon, and the two
routes of the Camino Real as they head toward Santo Domingo
Pueblo are visible here. Photo by author.*

The route up the face was primarily used by travelers on horse or mule because wagons would have had great difficulty ascending or descending such a steep road. This is the route that Zebulon Pike was taken on in 1807 on his way to Chihuahua and, finally, Louisiana.

Return to your car and drive on the north side of the river near the route of the acequia to the village of La Bajada, Pike's "small village," which still has a small chapel and a few modest homes. Continue through the village to the paved highway, where you will turn left and cross the river. The ruins of La Bajada Pueblo are to your left, adjacent to the river and across from the village of La Bajada. After cresting the hill (a few hundred yards after crossing the river), look to your right for the faint swales, evidence of the earliest camino.

Santo Domingo Pueblo to Bernalillo

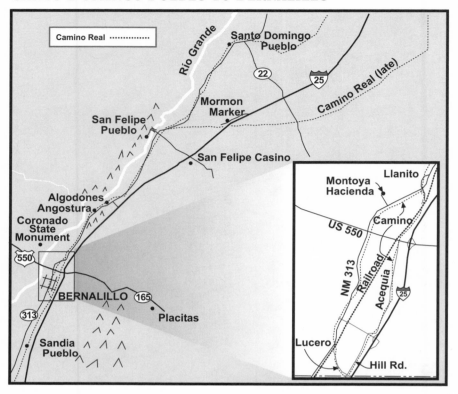

Continue to the stop sign at NM 16, then turn right toward Cochiti Pueblo. The next stop sign is at NM 22. Cochiti is to the right, but you need to turn left here, heading for Santo Domingo Pueblo. You'll pass through the small Hispanic community of Peña Blanca, which was sited in a small area between the lands granted to the Santo Domingo and Cochiti pueblos.

Santo Domingo Pueblo

Nearing the pueblo, you will cross over the wide arroyo formed by the Río Galisteo. The two caminos from La Bajada merged north of this arroyo and continued down the arroyo to the pueblo. Turn right into the pueblo (a historical marker is at the turn) and head for the large plaza. A church faces the plaza.

Santo Domingo Pueblo was the ecclesiastic capital of New Mexico. The Franciscans had their headquarters here, including their archives. During the

1680 Pueblo Revolt, three priests were killed at the pueblo. Tamarón, on his inspection tour in 1680, noted sixty-seven families here but no settlers. This lack of "settlers" was unusual, since Spanish citizens resided in many of the pueblos.

San Felipe Pueblo

From the south side of the very large plaza, a paved road leads to San Felipe Pueblo. The camino will follow a familiar pattern here, remaining just above the floodplain along the edge of the hills. The road is paved until it crosses the railroad tracks, where it becomes a good gravel road as far as San Felipe Pueblo. A marker, Pueblo of San Felipe, stands near the stop sign at the edge of the pueblo.

Almost every camino traveler commented on the pueblo of San Felipe. It lay across the Rio Grande on the west side of the river under an impressive mesa. Zebulon Pike wrote that "at the village of St. Philips we crossed the Rio Grande on a bridge of eight arches." A subsequent flood made short work of this bridge. Tamarón noted eighty-nine Indian families at San Felipe in 1760. You can use the modern bridge to cross the river about one mile upstream from the pueblo. The pueblo's site and situation lend it a real charm.

One feature that you can see here and, in fact, may have seen at the other pueblos is the little outdoor ovens scattered among the homes. These adobe ovens, called *hornos* in New Mexico, are a direct result of the Spanish intrusion. They are used to bake bread. Just a generation or two ago, Hispanic families in New Mexico also used the ovens, but today their use is confined almost entirely to the pueblos.

Cross back to the east side of the river and look for the paved road leading south (the continuation of the gravel road on which you entered the reservation). This road follows the camino more or less for the next few miles. You leave the pueblo lands about where the electric generating plant is.

Today the area immediately south of the San Felipe reservation is called Algodones, but it was likely known as Bernalillo in the eighteenth and nineteenth centuries. After de Vargas reoccupied New Mexico, Spanish settlements were in three areas: Santa Cruz, Santa Fe, and Bernalillo. Bernalillo was the settled area between the Keres-speaking Indians at San Felipe and the Tiwa-speaking Indians at Sandia Pueblo, south of modern Bernalillo.

Today Algodones, an attractive community, blends into the next community of Angostura. Angostura, or, as it was called earlier, La Angostura de Bernalillo, is the Spanish word for "narrows," for the narrow opening through which the river passes. This site was also an important river crossing because it has a good gravel bed. Everyone, Indians and Spaniards, would have utilized this crossing to travel

Floodplain

The Rio Grande has created a substantial floodplain as its water moved south to El Paso del Norte. Floodplains are created by deposition—a process that creates an almost perfectly flat surface. From the accompanying diagram of the river and floodplain in cross section, you can see the river's water passing over the natural levees bordering the stream and then depositing silt on the floodplain. The diagram represents the floodplain in its natural state before human intervention to control the river's path with man-made levees. Coarser material would have been deposited close to the river on the natural levees, with the finer clays in the basins.

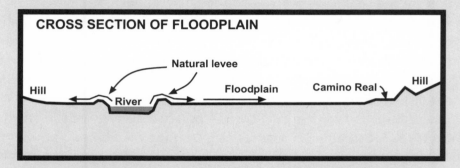

Periodically floods occurred, generally during the months of June and July, when the river's flow was increased by melting snow in the Sangre de Cristo and San Juan mountains to the north. This meant that the level floodplains were often water-filled soggy surfaces not suitable for cart or wagon use.

At times the river cut through the natural levees and pursued a new path, perhaps on the other side of the valley. Where the river's path is immediately adjacent to foothills, the camino would ascend the hills, making for a difficult patch. South of La Joya is the first of these diversions—such stretches were called *vueltas* by the Spaniards—turns, ascents, and descents over rough areas.

The Camino Real was situated on the east side—the left bank as you look downstream—just above the floodplain. Some descriptions said the camino was "at the edge of the sand hills." The camino north from San Juan Pueblo was in that position—it was at the edge of the hills. And so it will be, south from Santo Domingo Pueblo through Albuquerque and on to Fra Cristóbal, where the camino leaves the river for the Jornada del Muerto. And after the jornada, the camino once again continues its pattern of following the edge of the valley, from Fort Selden to El Paso del Norte. At El Paso, the camino used the ford, *vado* in Spanish, to cross the river, and from there it headed overland to Chihuahua.

to the western portion of the province. You will see a marker, La Angostura, on your right after you pass under the railroad tracks.

Beyond the narrows, you will pass into another Keres pueblo reservation, that of Santa Ana. Because the actual pueblo lay to the west, where the Río Jemez enters the Rio Grande, no traveler mentioned traveling through Santa Ana on the camino. Driving south, you will see a few houses on the reservation before entering Llanito, a Hispanic village. There you can turn right off NM 313 onto Llanito Road and pass a block or two on the camino through the village.

After rejoining NM 313, turn right, then immediately left on Edith. Follow Edith to its end (about one-quarter of a mile). This stretch, traveling parallel to the acequia, almost certainly follows the earliest camino route.

BERNALILLO

Return to NM 313 and turn left toward Bernalillo. At 0.3 mile, a sign on your right at Barros Road indicates the Hacienda Grande Bed and Breakfast. The B and B occupies the Montoya-Gallegos house, which was probably built immediately after the de Vargas entry. An Antonio Gallegos in this area married a Rosa Montoya; Antonio died in about 1715. The house is an enclosed structure with a central patio, or *placita*. The modest living quarters made up about half the structure, the balance being used for the farming operation.

Continue south on NM 313 until you reach a major intersection with traffic lights, where you should turn left (east) and drive up the hill toward the interstate. Just beyond a park-and-ride lot at a signal light, at a road marked South Hill, you should turn right. In about one-half mile you are back on the camino, with the acequia visible at some points to your right. This road follows the Camino Real almost continuously from here through Albuquerque.

Continue south on South Hill past the intersection with NM 473 (which intersects with the interstate just to your left). You will eventually reach a gate, one of the few breaks in the route, placed here by Sandia Pueblo to prevent traffic from entering the reservation at this point. You will pick up the camino later in the center of the pueblo.

Near the gate, a paved road goes west (right) from South Hill. Take this road and meander west until you arrive back at NM 313, Bernalillo's main street. The road you follow is variously called Los Arboles, Gutiérrez, and finally, as you make the turn to NM 313, Lucero. These roads follow what was a spur from the Camino Real for travelers having business in Bernalillo. Bernalillo, by early traveler accounts, stretched several miles north of Sandia Pueblo on both sides of

The old Montoya-Gallegos house in Bernalillo. Montoya-Gallegos House Photograph (photographer unknown), Bainbridge Bunting Collection, Center for Southwest Research, University Libraries, University of New Mexico.

the Rio Grande. Today the floodplain is almost entirely to the east of the river, which indicates that the Rio Grande has shifted course and moved west to its present location.

Originally called Real de Bernalillo, with the "Real" indicating that it was a mining town, Bernalillo's place in history is important, for it was one of three locales that had Spanish settlers immediately after the reconquest in the late seventeenth century. It was from Bernalillo that settlers went to found Albuquerque. It was also here that de Vargas died in 1704 while chasing a group of Apaches.

Reaching NM 313, called Camino del Pueblo here, turn right and continue through the community until you reach the intersection with US 550, the same intersection you were at earlier. Turn left (west) and continue on US 550, crossing the river. Look for signs on the right directing you to Coronado State Monument, on a road just a few hundred yards past the river crossing.

Coronado State Monument contains the ruins of the Tiwa pueblo called Kuaua. A short walk will take you through the pueblo, which includes a reconstructed kiva. A significant number of murals were found in this kiva, and many of them can be viewed today.

The name *Coronado* comes from the Spanish explorer Francisco Vásquez de Coronado, who entered New Mexico from the west in 1540 while searching for gold. Coronado and his men camped in this general area from 1540 to 1541. At that time, approximately eight Tiwa-speaking pueblos existed in this general area, four on each side of the Rio Grande. Of those, only two survive, Sandia and Ysleta, and you'll visit these later on your trip.

Return to Bernalillo and turn right onto Camino del Pueblo (NM 313). At the edge of town, on the left, is a marker, Bernalillo. Drive south on 313 as far as the crossroad to your left for Sandia Pueblo, just beyond mile marker 4. (A historical marker is on the highway at the second entrance to the pueblo if you want to see it.) Drive east on Sandia Loop until you come to a T. This road, called North Santa Fe Trail, is the Camino Real. If you turned left here (you should not) and followed it north, you would arrive at the gate you saw in southern Bernalillo, at the south end of South Hill Road.

Sandia Pueblo (called Tuf Shurn Tui by the Sandia people) had a convent in the 1630s, which remained important until 1680, when the Indians here joined in the revolt. At that time, the church was destroyed, but the padres were able to escape. By 1681 the Sandia Indians had fled to lands of the Hopis in present-day Arizona. When Pedro de Rivera on his inspection tour of frontier defenses passed through here in 1726, he saw only ruins of the pueblo, its inhabitants having fled.

Convinced by the Spanish to return, many of the Sandia Indians did so around 1748, bringing with them some Hopi (called Moqui at the time). Bishop Tamarón, on his inspection tour in 1760, noted fifty-one Tiwa families and sixteen Moqui families here. The two groups have blended together today, but some rituals practiced at Sandia are Hopi in origin.

Turn right at the intersection and you follow a road (it becomes South Santa Fe Trail after the stop sign) sandwiched between the acequia and the sand hills to the east. In a few miles, not far before leaving the reservation, to the east was another Tiwa pueblo called Puaray. The two padres in the Chamuscado expedition in 1581–82 decided to remain in Puaray when the balance of the expedition returned to Mexico. They were later killed here. This pueblo joined the revolt in 1680, but when de Vargas came through here in 1692, it was in ruins. No attempt was made to resettle it after the reconquest.

SANDIA PUEBLO TO ALBUQUERQUE

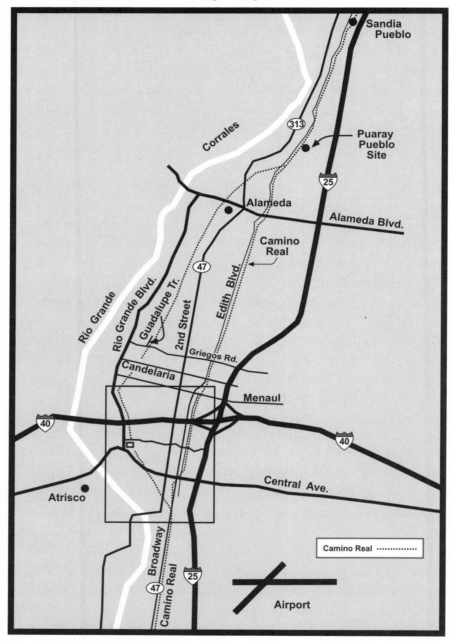

The road you have been traveling on, named Edith after exiting the pueblo, follows the usual pattern of hugging the sand hills. You have now passed into the community of Alameda, a name given by the Spaniards to a pueblo that was, at that early date, on the west side of the river. In the early 1600s, the river ran about where 2nd Street is today. It since has made several avulsions, or shifts, with the last major flood occurring in 1903.

At this point, you must make a choice. You can continue on Edith, following the colonial-era Camino Real, or you can drop down to Alameda and follow an alternate camino route.

First, the original route. Continue on Edith (named Bernalillo Road on early maps), paralleling the acequia, which is never very far from the road. When you reach Candelaria, you continue south but must jog around the Menaul School. You will come to a stoplight at Menaul Boulevard, where you should turn left, go east one long block to Edith, and turn right. Again you are following the camino and will remain on it until somewhere near Lomas, where the camino angled southwest to join today's Broadway. A nineteenth-century settlement was on the camino where it met Mountain Road, called Martineztown, and you will be passing through that community. You'll have to turn west at either Lomas or Central to reach Broadway. Now you can follow either Lomas or Central to the west, as either will take you to your next stop, at Old Town.

The second route requires you to drive west toward the river. To do this, you should turn right at Alameda Boulevard and drive downhill to 4th Street. Because the valley developed at the time Albuquerque was being made into a villa, other roads were established connecting the new communities. One historian notes that there were four small communities from Albuquerque to Alameda: Los Ranchos de Albuquerque, Los Griegos, Los Montoyas, and Los Gallegos. The last three were named in the usual manner of New Mexico: for the most prominent family in that community.

As you drive west on Alameda Boulevard, you will pass the Nativity of the Blessed Virgin Mary Catholic church on the southeast corner of Alameda and 4th Street. (You passed the old river channel at about 2nd Street.) Continue on Alameda to Rio Grande Boulevard (a signal light is here). The Tiwa pueblo of Alameda stood near this corner, as did the later colonial community of Alameda. Alameda Pueblo joined the 1680 revolt but was abandoned afterward. The returning Spaniards attempted to restart Alameda in 1702 with some fifty stray Tiwas. When this attempt failed, the remaining Indians were moved to Isleta Pueblo in 1708.

ALBUQUERQUE

Before the Pueblo Revolt in 1680, a string of *estancias* stretched from Angostura to Isleta. An estancia is a cattle ranch or large farm in today's Spanish, but in colonial times, it would likely have been a modest house and small ranch. One of these estancias was that of Francisco de Trujillo. Trujillo died in the 1760s, leaving his property to his wife, doña Luisa de Trujillo. Old Town Albuquerque sits about where the estancia of doña Luisa de Trujillo was. Like other estancias, the Trujillo place had been sited on slightly elevated ground to help protect against the annual Rio Grande floods. Immediately south of the Trujillo property was the Hacienda de Mejía, in an area called Esteros de Mejía. The term *esteros* means "estuaries," which tells us that the area was basically a swamp at certain times of the year.

This string of estancias was wiped out during the revolt, and the surviving settlers departed for El Paso del Norte and safety. After the return of the Spanish in 1693, the area was slowly reoccupied. At this time, the valley had only one more or less active pueblo, that of Isleta to the south. Settlers brought north with de Vargas occupied the area around today's Bernalillo first, with small ranches extending from Algodones to just north of Alameda Pueblo.

Acting governor Francisco Cuervo y Valdes chose the old Estancia de doña Luisa as the site for a new villa, the fourth to be so ordained in the province. In order of founding, they would be Santa Fe, El Paso del Norte, Santa Cruz de la Cañada, and Albuquerque. Certainly the province needed an administrative center for the growing population of the Río Abajo area, the region south of La Bajada. However, the circumstances surrounding the founding of the villa at Albuquerque were suspect. The governor, who was only "acting," apparently tried to court favor with the viceroy by naming the villa after him, don Francisco Fernández de la Cuerva Enríquez, Duke of Alburquerque (the first *r* has been subsequently dropped). The accepted date of founding was April 23, 1706.

Creating villas was a formal act with certain requirements. The location was to be salubrious, a certain population was required, and a formal villa plan (plaza, streets, blocks) had to be made. Cuervo told the viceroy that thirty-five families already lived in the new villa, when in truth probably only thirty-five families lived in the entire valley. You will visit other Spanish villas providing the required plans, such as Chihuahua, Durango, and later Querétaro, and obtain a better sense of what a plan entailed. Albuquerque really had no plan—it should be stated that neither did the other villas in the province. Albuquerque did have a church early on, built on the west side of a plaza called the Plaza de Armas, as many other villas called theirs. Behind the church were soldiers' barracks, called by some the presidio.

And the valley did need soldiers! The Comanches had become a major threat to the Spanish settlements by 1750. Taos had been attacked in 1760, as reported by Bishop Tamarón, and Albuquerque was visited by Comanches in June 1774. At that time, two hundred of these raiders attacked the villa, killing two residents and stealing the villa's stock.

Water for the many farms in and around the villa came from an acequia madre into which water was diverted from a dam several miles north of the villa. The acequia madre ran along the edge of the sand hills on the east, with laterals directing water to the farms below.

An early visitor to the area was Pedro de Rivera on his inspection of frontier defenses of 1726. Rivera reported that the population consisted of Spaniards, mestizos, and mulattos, who lived in dispersed ranchos in the valley. He had visited El Paso del Norte and would visit Santa Fe, two villas that clearly were much more important than Albuquerque. Rivera did not stay in the villa but camped in a *despoblado* (an unpopulated area) called Rosa de Castilla, near the river and only three miles north. Certainly if there had been much of a town, he would have stayed in it.

By 1750, 190 Spanish families lived in or near the villa, with another 200 Indians. Bishop Tamarón, in 1760, counted 270 families totaling 1,814 persons, a number that included people from across the river in an area known as Atrisco. A census taken in 1789 counted a population of 1,347, but this number was for the villa and the plazas up and down the valley that were dependent on the villa. It should be clear that not many residents were actually living "in" Albuquerque during the eighteenth century.

What kind of community was Albuquerque in the later colonial period? Spanish policy prevented trade with non-Spanish territories. This policy, called mercantilism, was to protect Spanish producers from competition. Outsiders who wandered into New Mexico, and some did, were arrested and sent south to Mexico City. This policy resulted in great hardship for residents of New Mexico. They were allowed to send woven goods, salt, and piñon nuts south in trade for what they needed. And prices for New Mexican exports and for imports from the south were determined by merchants in Chihuahua, who kept New Mexicans in their debt and impoverished.

The census of 1790 listed forty-seven weavers, twenty-five carders, and fifteen spinners in the Albuquerque area. These residents were producing goods for export south. A few shoemakers were also listed. Trade was largely through

ALBUQUERQUE

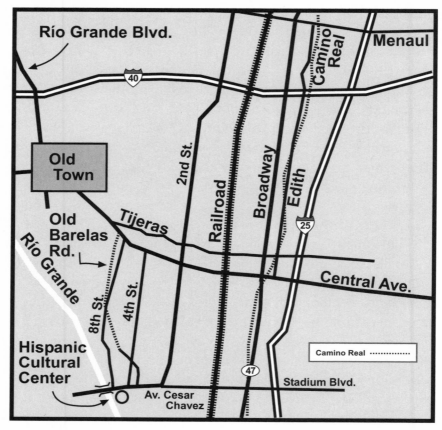

barter, with not much need for a merchant class. This situation did not change appreciably until Mexican independence in 1821 and the concomitant opening of the Santa Fe Trail to the United States.

Lieutenant Zebulon Pike offers the first outsider's view of Albuquerque in his description of a visit in 1807 to what he calls a village. He met with Father Ambrosio, who hosted a dinner for him. Pike had been captured north of Santa Fe and was being taken to Chihuahua when he arrived at the area in March, a time when the acequias were being repaired and cleaned. He was impressed with the "joyful labor" of the men, women, and children employed in their acequia work.

By 1822 Albuquerque was beginning to look like a town. A census that year listed 2,302 people living in the area around the town. The residents were mostly farmers, but fifteen were designated merchants, thirteen craftsmen, three

ALBUQUERQUE OLD TOWN

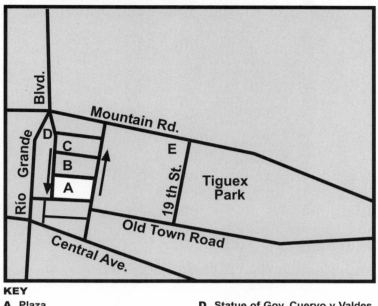

KEY

A Plaza

B San Felipe de Neri Church

C Store with terrones

D Statue of Gov. Cuervo y Valdes

E Albuquerque Museum

teachers, and one priest. This, of course, was just one year after Mexican independence and the opening of the Santa Fe Trail, whose impact was yet to be felt.

The Mexican era (1821–47) was one of dramatic change for the town. Traders coming to New Mexico on the Santa Fe Trail quickly glutted the market with American and European goods. The little currency available in New Mexico had gone east with the traders on their return trips for more goods. The traders, Americans and some New Mexicans, soon realized that they could continue south through Albuquerque to Chihuahua and beyond. This period became a golden age for the now fast-growing town. New Mexicans such as the Peréas, Chávezes, and Armijos became important and wealthy traders—both on the Santa Fe Trail and the now-renamed Camino Nacional, or Chihuahua Trail, to the south.

At the intersection of Alameda and Rio Grande, turn left and follow Rio Grande as it twists and turns in its route to Albuquerque. Twisting and turning almost always indicates that the road is an old one, predating any survey. The boulevard passes through a wealthy stretch of the valley with large homes, many with horse barns. As you drive south, look out for some of the names associated with early Albuquerque such as Candelaria, Griegos, and Gallego.

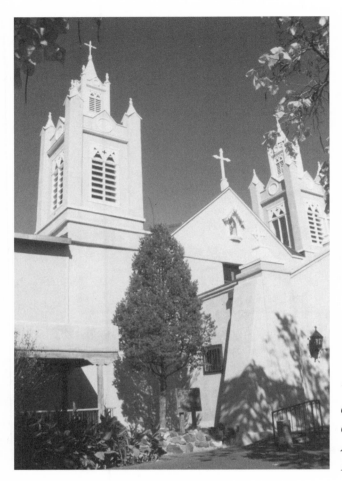

*The church of San Felipe
de Neri, built in 1793
on the old plaza in
Albuquerque.
Photo by author.*

The later camino connecting these communities left Old Town on present-day Rio Grande Boulevard, following it north to Griegos Road. As you are coming from the north, look for Griegos Road and turn left (east). After about one-half mile on Griegos, immediately after you pass over an acequia, turn left onto Guadalupe Trail. This road was once a branch of the camino. Bits and pieces of Guadalupe can be found north beyond Alameda Boulevard. The stretch of Guadalupe you are on is a particularly attractive piece of the old camino. After seeing it, return to Rio Grande Boulevard and go south.

Passing under Interstate 40, you will soon come to a stoplight at Mountain Road. It is best to turn left here (east) and drive two blocks to the Albuquerque Museum, where you will find adequate parking. You will certainly want to view the exhibits here as you begin your tour of old Albuquerque.

Rafael Armijo's store on the plaza in Albuquerque. Now a restaurant,
it was mentioned in Susan Magoffin's journal. Photo by author.

The Albuquerque Museum has a fine permanent display of artifacts from the precontact Indian, Spanish colonial, and Mexican eras. In addition, the museum hosts other displays on a temporary basis. Occasionally these displays relate to the Camino Real.

From the museum, a short walk takes you to the plaza of the San Felipe de Neri church. Recall that the first church was built on the west side of the plaza (to your left as you face the present church). When that adobe church collapsed in 1792, construction of the present church began almost immediately, in 1793. The church, however, has been remodeled many times, so you are not seeing it as it looked in 1793.

The restaurant La Placita on the southeast corner of the plaza is likely the site of a store operated in the 1840s by Rafael Armijo, a nephew of then governor Manuel Armijo. Susan Magoffin, who was accompanying her trader husband in 1846–47, mentioned stopping "for a few moments at the store of Don Raphel Armijo," going on to comment that "the store is very spacious, with wide portals in front."

From the plaza, walk north on either street to get to Church Street, behind the church. At 2113 Church Street, you will find a building of considerable age, but direct your attention to a small niche to the right of the entrance with a glass cover over it. The remodeler of this building some years ago left this opening so we might see the *terrones* that were used in the original construction. These blocks, or bricks, were cut directly out of the ground much as one cuts turf or peat. The many floods, with the accompanying sediment and plant growth, created a turf that when cut in blocks could be used in place of adobe bricks. Probably not as strong as adobe, the terrones may have been used in the early church and might help explain its collapse.

In a small triangular park at the intersection of Mountain and Rio Grande stands an equestrian statue of don Francisco Cuervo y Valdes, the acting governor who was instrumental in the founding of Albuquerque. The date of founding, April 23, 1706, is inscribed on the marker near the statue.

After visiting the old plaza area, leave by heading east on Central Avenue, the major road to the south of Old Town. Central was probably the main connecting branch of the Camino Real. Turn right at 8th Street. (You will cross Tijeras Avenue at the point that Central meets 14th Street. If you have in hand a detailed map of Albuquerque, you will see that Tijeras is crooked, not on the main north-to-south grid. Tijeras was the main thoroughfare from Old Town to Tijeras Canyon and beyond in early periods.) As you drive south on 8th Street, you are approximating the camino from Old Town to the main Camino Real. Continue on 8th to Cesar Chávez, where on the south side of the street, you will find the National Hispanic Cultural Center of New Mexico.

Cross over to the south side of Cesar Chávez and park your car in one of the large parking lots. The new Hispanic Cultural Center is well worth a visit. Besides exhibition halls and performance venues, it has two fine libraries. One is a research library, with most volumes in Spanish, while the other, open to the public, has a good collection of books on the Southwest, Mexico, and the Camino Real. After visiting the center, you should drive north on 4th Street (the street on the east side of the cultural center).

After one long block on 4th, you will see a street coming in from the right called Barelas. You are now in the Barelas neighborhood, and Barelas Street is the old camino as it left Barelas for Old Town. Turn left here to follow Barelas as it winds its way north. Today it ends at a community center, but it would have continued north to Old Town until at least the twentieth century. Return to 4th and Cesar Chávez.

After visiting the Hispanic Cultural Center, you should head south either of two ways. To follow the original Camino Real, go east on Cesar Chávez to Broadway (NM 47) and turn right (south) here to follow the route of the camino. New México 47 follows the general course of the camino for many miles to the south.

You can also leave the center, turn west on Cesar Chavez, and follow NM 314 (which is part of old Route 66) south to Isleta Pueblo. This latter road follows a road used in the late-colonial and Mexican periods as communities began to grow on the west side of the Rio Grande. If you decide on this route, you can rejoin the text at Isleta Pueblo since NM 314 passes the pueblo.

Between Albuquerque and Isleta, the camino followed its usual pattern, above the floodplain and below the sand hills. Two named places were to be found in this stretch. Adolph Wislizenus, a scientist-doctor accompanying a Santa Fe Trail trader in 1846, wrote that he halted two miles south of Albuquerque at Sandival's (Sandoval) hacienda. The hacienda was situated on an upper and drier road, according to him. Eliot Coues, Pike's editor, describes Sandival's hacienda as well. Pike himself, however, who went south on the road west of the river, doesn't mention Sandival's hacienda. The map drawn in 1847 by Lieutenant James W. Abert, a topographical surveyor in the U.S. Army, has a location on it he calls "Placeres," which, in distance anyway, would be about where the mysterious Sandival's hacienda was supposed to have been. Both are lost to us today, and driving south on Broadway, you may wish for something to see in that industrial landscape.

ISLETA PUEBLO

You are driving parallel to Interstate 25, then eventually you pass over it and see the Isleta casino on your left. You have entered the Isleta Reservation, today the southernmost of the pueblos. Continue south about 3.5 miles past the interstate and take the paved road to the right that quickly passes over the river and enters the pueblo of Isleta. Turn left at any one of several streets to arrive at the church and plaza.

Isleta Pueblo received its name as a result of its location at a point where the river at times split just north of the pueblo and came together again south of it. This split made the pueblo, for at least part of the time, a little island, or *isleta* in Spanish. Isleta, then as now, was on the west side of the Rio Grande. However, most travelers on the camino mention the pueblo, and many camped nearby and crossed the river to visit it.

Isleta residents did not join the Pueblo Revolt in 1680, perhaps a result of the pueblo's isolation. After the revolt, Governor Antonio de Otermín returned

ALBUQUERQUE TO TOMÉ

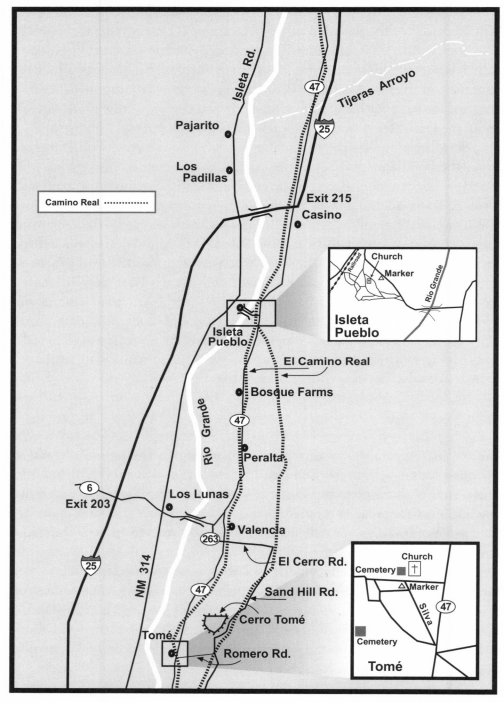

*Church at Isleta Pueblo, probably the oldest church in New Mexico.
Photo by author.*

in 1681–82 to assess the situation in the province. As he returned south through Isleta, he took about four hundred Isletans with him. This group of Tiwa Indians would form the nucleus of the new pueblo Ysleta del Sur (south) near El Paso del Norte, which Otermín directed to be established. You will visit this Texas pueblo, which still functions, when you are in El Paso. Apparently not all the Tiwas were gathered up by Otermín because the original Isleta Pueblo survived. The small group there was augmented by Tiwas from the failed attempt at restarting Alameda Pueblo north of Albuquerque.

The church San Agustín de la Isleta, dating from 1613 and likely the oldest church in New Mexico, was partially destroyed twice but was rebuilt on the same foundations in about 1709. When Pedro de Rivera passed by in 1726, he noted a small number of Tiwa Indians at the pueblo but did not mention the church. Bishop Tamarón, in 1760, mentioned the citizens of Isleta meeting him but did not describe the pueblo or church. The church farther south in Tomé relied on the priest in Albuquerque in 1760, so the pueblo may also have. However, Nicolás de Lafora, on his inspection in 1766, mentions La Isleta on the other side of the river and says it had a Franciscan priest. This may have been one result of Tamarón's visit.

Pueblo Decline

Of the many things the Spanish brought with them when they explored and conquered New Mexico, none had a greater impact than disease. Residents of the New World had no immunity to the diseases of the Old World. Some adults might survive an epidemic, but children born later would lack the immunity, and many of these would later succumb to the same disease. Almost every surviving adult bore the pockmarks left from smallpox.

The accompanying map gives an indication of the dramatic decline in pueblos and, by inference, population during the first century of Spanish occupation. When Coronado entered New Mexico in 1540, about one hundred thousand natives resided in some one hundred pueblos. In 1600, when Oñate brought his settlers, pueblo numbers were already down to eighty-one and the population to sixty thousand.

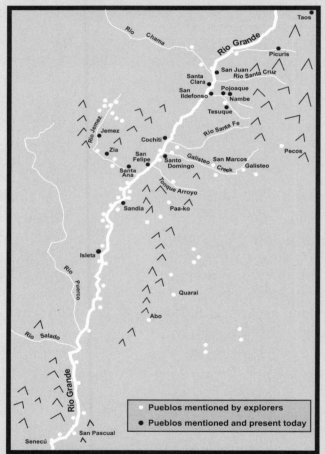

Several factors help explain the decimation in New Mexico. Certainly the labor requirements imposed by the Spanish added to the customary droughts, helped to weaken communities, and led to famine. The declines were particularly noted in the south, in the Piro and Tompiro pueblos.

The Peublo decline, based on a map in Elinore M. Barrett's Conquest and Catastrophe: Changing Rio Grande Pueblo Settlement Patterns in the Sixteenth and Seventeenth Centuries

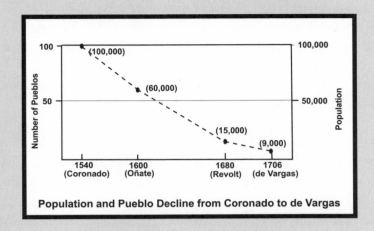

Population and Pueblo Decline from Coronado to de Vargas

Probably the largest single killer was smallpox. This disease, called *"el peste"* in New Mexico, had already killed millions in central Mexico. Other Old World diseases that had an impact were measles, dysentery, and typhoid. Elinore Barrett, a historical geographer, noted that the smallpox epidemic recorded in Zacatecas, Monterrey, and Parral in the period 1636–38 likely moved north with the caravans into New Mexico. This might explain the significant population declines in the northern province in about 1640. Barrett wrote that from 1629 to 1641, population decreased by 68 percent and the pueblos in this province by half (the map is a result of her research).

The decline continued until, in 1680, the year the Pueblo Revolt began, the numbers were thirty-one pueblos and fifteen thousand population. The Puebloan people may have realized that they had to act promptly to survive. Just after the reconquest, 1706, the numbers were nine thousand Indians living in nineteen pueblos, mostly the pueblos we see today. The Spanish entrada had truly been a catastrophe for the Indians of New Mexico.

As mentioned earlier, such population losses occurred throughout New Spain. Entire communities were lost on the coastal plains, and dramatic declines took place in the central highlands. Some losses, of course, were a result of Spanish mistreatment and warfare, but the Spanish rulers seemed as baffled by the decline as anyone. The decline meant fewer laborers for the farms and mines and was clearly not to their benefit. In the case of smallpox, the vaccine for protection made its way into the New World early in the nineteenth century, shortly after its development in England. A crash program of vaccination moved north along the Camino Real to reach New Mexico, and by 1810 the threat of smallpox was virtually ended.

Return to NM 47 and turn right (south). As you crossed the river, you likely noted the large diversion dam. A few of these very large structures have sup-
planted the many small community dams (*presas*) used in the past. The new
system of storage and diversion also has made the Rio Grande go dry in many
stretches.

Immediately on leaving the reservation, you enter Bosque Farms, an area
settled as a result of the shift of the Rio Grande in 1769 to its present position
two miles west. Before that date, scant farmland would have existed on this
side of the river because the sand hills come close to the highway today. This
area was home to the Chávez family, with José Mariano Chávez owning a
hacienda in the area by 1800, adjacent to NM 47 on the east between Pine and
Abo streets.

The Civil War battle of Peralta occurred in this area. Confederate soldiers, forced to retreat south from Glorieta (east of Santa Fe) in April 1862,
were attacked at the Chávez hacienda. This skirmish was the last fought in
New Mexico; afterward, the Confederates split up and made as best they could
for Texas.

Continue south on NM 47, watching for the church on your right. This
church, Our Lady of Guadalupe, faced the plaza of Peralta. The Otero family
had a hacienda here, which was situated to the immediate south of the church.
Peralta is a later community since it was not mentioned by Rivera when he
passed through in 1726.

Continue south on NM 47 toward Valencia, where an estancia once stood
under the ownership of Francisco de Valencia but was destroyed in the time of
the revolt. When Rivera came through, he stayed here at what he called the
despoblado (unpopulated) Valencia. The church, Sangre de Cristo, will be on
your right as you enter the community. Seventeen families lived here in 1777,
but this church had not yet been built.

Valencia had two plazas, with one at the present church site, about where
the estancia and an earlier pueblo stood. The second plaza is south of this location, at the intersection of NM 47 and North El Cerro Loop. Look for this
road as you continue south on NM 47 and turn left at North El Cerro, which is
also NM 263.

Drive on North El Cerro, approaching the sand hills, until you come to
Sand Hill Road, where you turn right (south). You are now on the earlier
Camino Real that passed to the east of Cerro Tomé, your next stop. During
this early period, the Rio Grande ran adjacent to the *cerro* (hill), so the camino
was in its usual position at the edge of the sand hills.

Cerro Tomé, south of Los Lunas on the Camino Real. Photo by author.

TOMÉ

The better-paved road, NM 263, will branch to your right before reaching Cerro Tomé, but you should stay left on Sand Hill Road. You will pass adjacent to the cerro on its east and then bend right before reaching a small park to your left. Ten small historical tablets are in the park as well as a large sculpture, *La Puerto del Sol*. As you leave the park, turn left on La Entrada Road to continue on the old camino. At Romero Road, just past a short patch of dirt road, turn right and drive back to NM 47 to visit the village of Tomé.

Tomé is situated on NM 47 and astride the later variant of the Camino Real. The first settler in the area was Tomé Dominguez, who had an estancia here before the revolt, probably very near the cerro. The Dominguez family left for El Paso del Norte with the balance of the refugees and did not return with de Vargas. Tomé was resettled in about 1740 as a frontier town. Many of the first settlers were genízaros, the same class that had settled in Ojo Caliente and Abiquiu in the north.

Visitors to Tomé included Bishop Tamarón in 1760, who remarked that Tomé was a new town, with a "decent church" already built. The bishop confirmed 402 persons while there. At this time, Tomé did not have a resident priest but relied on visitations by the priest from Albuquerque. Lafora, just a few years after Tamarón, noted many changes in this area. He counted seventy residents in Tomé, or the Pueblo of La Limpia Concepción, as he called it.

Cross over NM 47 to visit the church in Tomé, named Our Lady of the Conception and about one-half mile west of NM 47. The town may have been a fortified plaza because defense was needed. Comanche attacks in May 1777 and June 1778 cost fifty-one lives in the Tomé area.

Once again drive south on NM 47 and note the point where the highway passes close by the bluff on your left. The oldest variant of the camino would have headed for the cerro at this place. The camino is probably to your right as you pass by (it is visible from the air) because the highway is on a cut. In a few miles, NM 47 intersects with NM 309, which crosses the Rio Grande heading to Belen. Just past this intersection watch for NM 47 to veer left to continue to US 60 and Mountainair. You instead should take NM 304 south and along the river. Be careful, since it is easy to miss this junction.

Just after NM 304 crosses the railroad tracks, you will see a historical marker on your right, Las Barrancas. A prerevolt hacienda here, according to one source, was owned by the Robledo family. Another source says the Gómez family owned it. In any case, it was never reoccupied after the revolt.

The next stop is at a location called Casa Colorada, just a few miles beyond Las Barrancas. Very likely an early estancia stood in this area too. Rivera, on his inspection tour up the valley in 1724, noted many ruined haciendas and stock estancias in the route between Sevilleta (La Joya) and Valencia.

Tamarón, coming north on the Camino Real, says that "we passed the house they call Colorada, in ruins, and from that point on we began to see pens of ewes, corrals, and small houses." Thus it was that Casa Colorada formed the southern limit of occupation by 1760. But life was challenging for the settlers, with almost constant threats from Indian raiders, Apache and Comanche. A marker on the left in Casa Colorada states that the community was founded in the 1740s but also says it was later abandoned because of Apache attacks and not resettled until 1823.

Drive south on NM 304 to the small community of Veguita. There you will see a post office to your right and, just beyond the San Juan Mission and across the highway, the cemetery. No mention was made of this location in colonial times.

The next community on NM 304 is Las Nutrias. Otermín called this location

La Vega de las Nutrias (a *vega* is a meadow, and *nutrias* are beavers). Otermín, who was coming south with refugees from Santa Fe, caught up with refugees from the Río Abajo under Maestro de Campo Alonso García at this place. In 1766 Lafora wrote of thirty families living in Las Nutrias, all in skin huts.

You will be approaching US 60 when you leave Las Nutrias. Stop at the sign at US 60, then cross over the highway and continue south on NM 304. You will return to this spot later. In the first mile, you will be passing the site of the estancia of Felipe Romero, an important spot mentioned by almost every early trail user. When Tamarón passed it, he called it "the ruined estancia of Felipe Romero" and "lost with the kingdom." By that, he meant that it had been destroyed during the Pueblo Revolt in 1680. The estancia was likely situated on the bluff between NM 304 and the valley to your right.

La Joya de Sevilleta

La Joya de Sevilleta is your last stop on NM 304, for the highway ends at that community. This area is first mentioned by Juan de Oñate in 1598, when he called the Piro pueblo near here Nueva Sevilleta (New Seville). The pueblo site is on the bluff just a mile north of present-day La Joya. The first pueblo in which Oñate found it necessary to take refuge, this pueblo was important enough to have a convent and priest in the seventeenth century.

Piro residents of Sevilleta went south with Otermín when he retreated to El Paso del Norte in 1680. The Piro population from Sevilleta and a few other pueblos in the south settled in the new communities in El Paso del Norte called San Lorenzo and Socorro. The pueblo here was destroyed in the revolt in 1680 and not rebuilt. Again Tamarón described it in 1760 as "lost to the kingdom."

The ruins of the pueblo must have been substantial and very visible from the Camino Real because both Rivera in 1724 and Lafora in 1766 mention passing them. La Joya, the present community, was founded in the 1790s by landless farmers from the northern part of the province. It had a fortified plaza by 1800, and when Pike passed through in 1807, he was very impressed with the village, calling it "the neatest most regular village I have yet seen." Since La Joya was the last community before one reached El Paso del Norte, it was a collection point for caravans forming to enter the dangerous Jornada del Muerto.

You will see a marker, La Joya, on your right as you enter the village. Beyond the marker, you come to a road, actually, the Camino Real, where you should turn right and immediately look to your left for the church and plaza. The camino in this area (from US 60 to this location) ran just below the

SOUTH TO LA JOYA

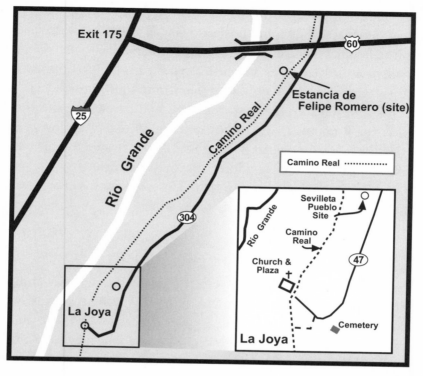

bluffs. After visiting the plaza, you can drive south through the village until you reach a fence. That identifies the border of the Sevilleta Land Grant, which is now the Sevilleta National Wildlife Refuge. From here the camino passed through the later villages of Joyita and Sabino before reaching Pueblito. You'll pick up the camino again at Pueblito.

Return north on NM 304 from La Joya to US 60. Turn west on US 60 and cross the Rio Grande, continuing to the interstate. Take the southbound ramp toward Socorro and continue on the interstate. Twelve miles south, you will see a prominent hill on your left (east) toward the river, San Acacia Butte. New Mexico is surveyed from a monument on the summit of this prominence. Called the "initial point," it is less than a mile from the small community of San Acacia.

Somewhere in the vicinity of San Acacia stood the Piro pueblo of Alamillo, abandoned during the Pueblo Revolt in 1680. The ruins of Alamillo were noted by many early Spanish travelers, including Otermín, de Vargas, and Bishop Tamarón. A small village called Alamillo now exists near San Acacia, but it is not

A New Mexico state historic marker at La Joya. Markers such as these are found along highways and rest stops throughout New Mexico. Photo by author.

known exactly where the pueblo was. The Arroyo de Alamillo, on the east side south of this point, may indicate that the pueblo was nearby.

Leave the interstate at the Escondido exit (Exit 152) and pass under the freeway, continuing through the hamlet of Escondido and turning left at a sign directing you to Escondida Lake. At 1.3 miles, turn right and pass over the Rio Grande to the even smaller community of Pueblito. Here you are back on the route of the camino.

The camino north of here passed over two bad stretches called *vueltas*. The northernmost was the Vuelta de Alamillo, and the one just to the north of Pueblito was Parida Hill. Travelers stayed on the edge of the floodplain where they could, but sometimes the river ran up to the very edge of the hills. When this happened, the travelers had to ascend the hills. These vueltas were written about by every colonial traveler.

Pueblito to Fra Cristóbal

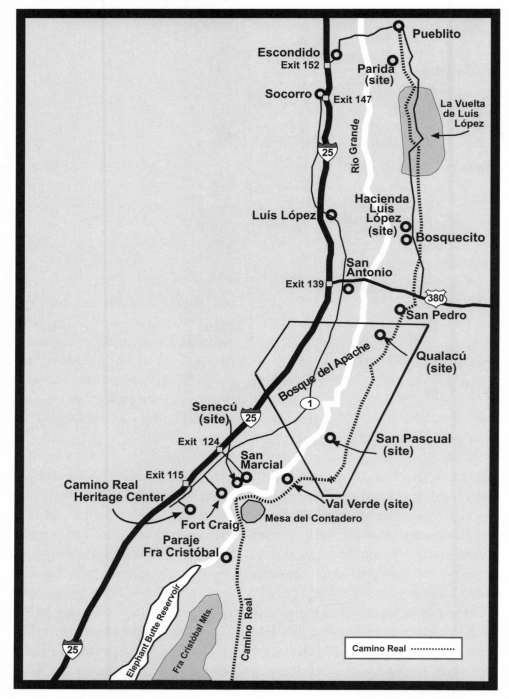

Continuing south from Pueblito, where the road is probably following directly on the camino, you may encounter a few sandy patches, but the road is reasonably well maintained south to NM 30 (seventeen miles). At 0.7 mile from Pueblito, you will find a road from the east marked by the Bureau of Land Management as Back Country Byway.

Just beyond this junction, on the river side of the road, is the site of Parida. Gregg described the camino in this area as traversing "upland ridges and undulating sections." Although the camino generally traversed the very edge of the valley, sometimes, because of wet or sandy conditions, it was forced up onto the ridges. You will experience these conditions between Pueblito and NM 380.

In the mid-1840s, Parida was the last town on the eastern side of the river, Socorro the last on the west side, before travelers reached Doña Ana, over one hundred miles south.

The stretch of the camino you are following south from Parida was often called La Vuelta de Luís López. Luís López had a seventeenth-century prerevolt hacienda at the south end of the vuelta, which you will be passing shortly. The northern end of this bad stretch lay opposite Socorro. Oñate reached this point on June 14, 1598, and received aid from the natives of the Piro pueblo of Teypana, across the river. They provided Oñate's caravan with food they badly needed, and he gave the community the name *Socorro*, meaning "relief" or "aid" in English. You will catch glimpses of the thriving community of Socorro across the river to the west along this stretch of the camino. During the 1840s, many American traders mentioned stopping at a paraje across from Socorro and fording the Rio Grande to visit the town.

Coming from the south, Bishop Tamarón mentions the site called Luís López. The following day, the good bishop had a mishap that is both humorous and informative. Leaving the López area on the seventeenth, Tamarón writes that he "went over a road full of ravines, and in one of them the *volante* (carriage) in which I and the Father Custos were riding suffered a severe upset. Father Custos fell from the side and received a blow that hurt him. I escaped injury, because I fell on him. Therefore, I took a horse and continued my journey on it." Tamarón never mentions Father Custos after this, so we'll never know how he survived the bishop's landing.

Continuing south, you arrive at pavement once again, at today's Bosquecito (little forest). Luís López's estancia was situated near the point where the pavement begins, on both sides of the river. The Mexican-era west-side community of Luís López gives testimony to the earlier settlement, the southernmost of many such settlements before the revolt.

In this area, Susan Magoffin describes her stay of some three months in late 1846 and early 1847. She mentions that she and her husband were living in the house of don José. She calls the locale San Gabriel in one section and Bosquito (should be Bosquecito) in another. The traders were staying here waiting for the American army to move farther south and into Chihuahua. On January 28, 1847, the Magoffins continued their trek southward. By this date, the army had defeated Mexican forces at Brazito and moved unopposed into El Paso del Norte.

Continue south over rolling hills to US 380, where you will turn right (west). Just after turning, you will find a New Mexico state marker, San Pedro, on your left. San Pedro, almost directly on the camino, was established on the east side of the Rio Grande probably around 1850. Leaving the marker site, you should continue west on US 380 to a road coming in from the left that will take you to San Pedro.

A few occupied buildings remain of San Pedro. At a T at the south end of the community, you can turn left and rejoin the camino for a mile or two. You will have to stop and return when you reach the Bosque del Apache Wildlife Refuge. From this point, the camino continues south on the east side of the river and can't be followed directly until we rejoin it at Engle, east of Truth or Consequences.

Return from San Pedro to US 380, then turn left (west), crossing the Rio Grande to the small town of San Antonio. You will see the Owl Café on the northwest corner of US 380 and NM 1. Today San Antonio is a stop for visitors to the Bosque del Apache Wildlife Refuge who need gasoline or food. The community does have a famous son, Conrad Hilton, and as you drive south on NM 1, you will pass by the remains of his first hotel. Hilton, of course, went on to create one of the world's largest hotel chains. Actually, this was his father's boardinghouse, which he inherited and which later became a hotel. The stone piles and partial walls can be seen about one-half mile south of US 380 on the right, just past a building marked Crystal Palace.

Continue south on NM 1, passing through the Bosque del Apache National Wildlife Refuge. The camino at this point lies across the river to the east. Three miles past the entrance signs to the bosque, there was an important Piro pueblo across the river. Oñate rested at this pueblo, Qualacú, in 1598. The pueblo residents fled at Oñate's approach, but a few were encouraged to return. Oñate and his troops camped here for a month outside the pueblo. Qualacú was abandoned by 1680, as were all the southern pueblos.

At mile marker 39, immediately after the Bosque del Apache exit sign on the left, you can see the Little San Pascual Mountains to your left across the river.

There a Piro pueblo, San Pascual, was situated, at the southern end of the Little San Pascual Mountains.

Continuing south on NM 1, you will see a historical marker, Mesa del Contadero, at mile marker 37. This mesa is the flat-topped volcanic mass across the river.

The next important camino site, again on the east side and therefore inaccessible to us, is Val Verde. Originally called Contadero because of the nearby Mesa de Contadero, this location was noted by Otermín. It was a paraje of long standing, a village at other times, and later (1862) the site of the Battle of Valverde between Union and Confederate forces. Valverde was a natural fording place and was used for this purpose throughout the camino period. Gregg and Wislizenus both mentioned the paraje at Valverde and noted that it was a deserted Mexican village.

NM 1 approaches Interstate 25 at Exit 124, where a gravel road from this exit crosses NM 1 and continues to the river at San Marcial. At the northeast corner of the intersection, a marker placed by the United Daughters of the Confederacy commemorates the role of the Texas Mounted Volunteers at the Battle of Valverde. It is about two miles from the marker to the site of San Marcial. San Marcial was destroyed by floods in the last century. Somewhere near the point where the road tees is the site of Senecú, the southernmost Piro pueblo, although so far, archaeologists have failed to locate the exact site. Oñate reached the first Piro village, which he called Trenequel, on May 28, 1598. He did not cross the river to Senecú but continued north to Qualacú, mentioned previously. The Spanish established a mission at Senecú, and a padre from Senecú established the first mission at Paso del Norte (El Paso del Norte, today's Ciudad Juárez, Mexico). Some of the residents of Senecú went south with Otermín in 1680 and were resettled at a new "Senecú" in Paso del Norte. Today the latter is a suburban community in Ciudad Juárez, Mexico.

From San Marcial, return to NM 1 and turn left in about seven miles, where a gravel road will be to your left. Take it for a short drive to Fort Craig. The remains of Fort Craig are 4.5 miles from NM 1. The site is maintained by the Bureau of Land Management, and a volunteer lives on the site to protect it. Fort Craig, begun in 1854 as a way of controlling raids by Apaches and Navajos on camino traders and nearby towns, was closed in 1885.

The most important event that occurred at Fort Craig took place in 1862, when a force of twenty-five hundred Confederate soldiers under General H. H. Sibley met a Union force at Valverde, north of Fort Craig on the east side of the river. Considered a Confederate victory, the battle did not help the supply-poor

Confederates, who lost many horses and supplies. Kit Carson was one of the commanders of the Hispanic troops, winning a commission of brevet general at Valverde. The site is worth a visit, with detailed descriptive brochures available in a kiosk at the parking lot.

Again return to NM 1, turn left, and drive past a gasoline station with café near Exit 115. Continue past the café one mile to a point where a rest stop is situated for the interstate. Turn left here and drive two miles to the new Camino Real Heritage Center, a joint effort by the Bureau of Land Management and the Museum of New Mexico. Construction of the center was completed in 2003, and it opened to the public in November 2005. The site itself is worth a visit, with Fra Cristóbal range looming to the southeast and the camino heading off from there to the Jornada del Muerto. To the northeast, one can just make out the low-lying Mesa del Contadero, already discussed.

Return to NM 1, turn right, and go back to the café at Exit 115 to rejoin the interstate heading south. From this point to the resort community of Truth or Consequences, you won't have much to see. One thing you will notice is the large number of substantial arroyos, or canyons, that the highway crosses. These arroyos partially explain why the camino did not follow the river here.

CHAPTER THREE

Jornada del Muerto through El Paso del Norte

✛   ✛   ✛

JORNADA DEL MUERTO

Use Exit 79 at Truth or Consequences, turn left, and go toward the center of town. At the traffic light, turn left onto NM 51, which will take you seventeen miles to Engle and back on the Camino Real. After turning east on NM 51, you will pass the dam that stores water in Elephant Butte Reservoir. Completed in 1916, this project allowed the Rio Grande to be channeled downstream through the Las Cruces and El Paso areas. With completion of the dam came stability to the Mesilla Valley, the valley downstream from the dam, since afterward floods were mostly avoided and the impact of droughts ameliorated.

Climbing out of the Rio Grande valley, you eventually reach a divide and begin the descent into the jornada route. The crossroads community of Engle appears in front of you where NM 51 meets the railroad. As you descend, you will see a New Mexico state marker on the right—very difficult to read—telling about the Jornada del Muerto. A separate brass plate commemorates the Cuarto-centenario, the four hundred years since Oñate's entrada in 1598.

Somewhere in this vicinity was the body of water that travelers called the Laguna del Muerto. The problem is that many candidates near here vie for this

Jornada del Muerto

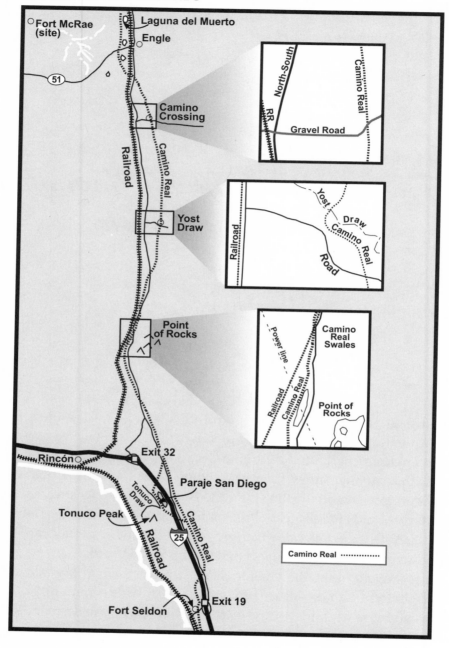

title. The map shows several, and we may never know which was "the" Laguna del Muerto. The usual strategy developed by travelers was to utilize the water in the *laguna* if there was any or unhitch the draft animals to take them west down the arroyo to the Ojo del Muerto. This *ojo*, or "spring," was found five miles west from the Camino Real. The later Fort McRae was situated at this spring or nearby. The jornada map shows the fort (Ojo del Muerto), several possible lagunas, and the several arroyos leading toward the ojo.

Fort McRae, established in 1863 and closed in 1876, was built to protect travelers on the camino from Apache marauders, on a site chosen at Ojo del Muerto, where a dependable water source was available.

Continuing from the jornada marker, you cross the camino about one mile before the railroad tracks. There a closed, fancy gate on your left marks the approximate crossing point. Beyond the gate, you will find a lake bed and yet another to your right and beyond the vineyard. Continue to Engle at the crossroads just across the railroad tracks. The camino north of here traverses private land and thus is inaccessible to the public.

Laguna del Muerto

Don't be disappointed about the closed northern portion, because there is plenty to see south of here. You will certainly get a feeling for the emptiness of the Jornada del Muerto. The road south is paved for five miles and then becomes a well-maintained gravel road with limited traffic. A substantial number of ranches are found between Engle and the interstate, thirty-eight miles south of here.

As you head south from Engle, the camino is on your right (west) and remains to the right for about 3.5 miles. The writer has attempted without success to locate the camino where it crosses the road. Farther south, after the road drops to cross an arroyo at Jornada Lakes (more candidates for the "Laguna del Muerto"), a gravel road crosses the north-south road. Turn left (east) onto this road and follow it 0.6 mile to a point where the camino crosses (see inset map). You'll have to park your vehicle and walk up and over the road, but you will see the faint trace on the north, a clearing of sorts through the underbrush. After you find it on the north side, you will see it on the south as well.

Return to the north-south road and turn south again, noting your odometer reading, and at 6.8 miles, you are at the approximate location of the paraje of Alemán. *Alemán* means "German" and probably refers to Bernardo Gruber, a trader from Sonora who was the subject of an inquisition in 1668. He escaped captivity and headed south only to die near this location. La Jornada del Muerto, the

Jornada del Muerto

Camino Real travelers, certainly those with carts and wagons, used a shortcut from the paraje at Fra Cristóbal to the paraje at Robledo (today's Fort Selden). This shortcut, still a distance of ninety miles, became known as the Jornada del Muerto, the journey of the dead man. Of the several possible explanations for the dead man referred to, the most likely candidate is the story of German trader Bernardo Gruber. Gruber was being held prisoner as a result of an inquisition transgression near Sandia Pueblo when, in 1668, he escaped and headed south along the camino. He was later found dead on the camino south of Engle, a place forever known as Paraje del Alemán (*Alemán* means "German" in Spanish). Gruber is likely to be the dead man referred to.

Juan de Oñate pioneered this route in 1598. Leaving the Rio Grande at what became known as Robledo's paraje, he went north, hoping to find water along the route. Others followed, and by 1700 the present trace was the accepted route. Water is scarce in the jornada but actually no more scarce than elsewhere in New Mexico. Two weather stations in the jornada area each report about nine inches of annual precipitation, almost all of which comes in July, August, and September. That is dry, of course, but nine inches is what the rest of the area gets as well. There is no permanent surface water, however, which makes it seem even drier.

Travelers developed strategies to thwart the challenges of aridity here. Leaving the paraje at Robledo, they would make the short day's trip to the paraje at San Diego. This paraje was on the very edge of the plain and looked down at the Rio Grande, several hundred feet below. The livestock would be sent down to the river to shorten the waterless stretch by one day. Likewise, when travelers reached the Laguna del Muerto (near today's Engle), they would send their livestock five miles west through a canyon to the Ojo del Muerto, a dependable spring. Later, in the eighteenth and nineteenth centuries, the ojo became a dependable source of Apache attacks. Then in 1863, Fort McRae was established near the Ojo de Muerto to protect the Camino Real travelers.

Two other jornadas are on the Camino Real, both in the Mexican state of Chihuahua. One lies south of here between El Paso del Norte (Ciudad Juárez today) and Laguna de los Patos. The other is south of Ojo Caliente. These other two jornadas did not present the challenge that the Jornada del Muerto did since they were considerably shorter.

journey of the dead man, may be named for Gruber and his death. By the 1700s, the jornada name was common.

As you continue south, with the camino remaining to your left, the next opportunity to see it comes at Yost Draw. At about two miles, a dirt road enters from the east. Take this road and drive 1.5 miles with Yost Draw on your left as you head east (see figure inset). Here, where the camino climbed out of the draw, you can detect traces of it. Bureau of Land Management archaeologists completed several excavations in this general area, and as a result, the camino is well documented here.

Point of Rocks

Return to the north-south road and turn left (south) again. The next location where one can see the camino is easier to get to. Continue about ten miles south to a point where the rails and the road begin to part (see figure inset). The camino here lies between the rails and the road. The camino had multiple paths in this area. After the rails and road part, drive a quarter of a mile and park. Walk toward the tracks and look for the multiple swales of the camino. The camino continues south from here to the west of Point of Rocks, which is to your left front and rises some few hundred feet above the road.

On the right side of the road, with Point of Rocks on your left, you will see a low outlier of rocks that shelters the camino from view. The camino is on the other side, to the west of the outlier, almost adjacent to the railroad tracks. Power lines crossing the road will orient you here. You can stop and follow the power lines to the right, and on arriving at the summit of the outlier, you can see the camino and tracks below you. Actually, traders who named this place "Point of Rocks" were likely referring to the outlier and not the small range to the east. (In similar fashion, traders on the Santa Fe Trail had named several locations in Kansas and New Mexico "Point of Rocks," an aiming point for their caravan.)

The Paraje del Perrillo was somewhere in the vicinity of Point of Rocks. The name *perrillo*, "little dog" in Spanish, is just one of the many place-names resulting from Oñate's 1598 journey. In this area, Oñate's caravan was desperate for water, and because it was May, before the rainy season had begun, the arroyos and ponds were all dry. One of the dogs accompanying the caravan wandered off, then returned with muddy paws. Retracing the dog's steps led to two water holes whose exact location is unknown today.

From Point of Rocks, continue south until you reach a fork (about five miles from the power lines), the better road going to the right, the poorer one leading straight ahead. On your left will be a concrete block building. The next

The Camino Real can be seen here near Point of Rocks in the
Jornada del Muerto. Photo by author.

important site is the Paraje San Diego, near the interstate. The jornada map
indicates two ways to find the paraje. Driving straight will let you follow the
route of the camino, and eventually you will parallel the interstate. You can also
arrive at the paraje by taking the right branch here and reaching the interstate at
the Upham exit.

Paraje San Diego

Driving straight, you are on the camino, and at about nine miles you will come
to the interstate and an underpass that you need to take. As you approach the
interstate, you will see Tonuco Mountain, which looms over the Rio Grande.
Going through the underpass, you immediately come to a cattle gate. Go
through it, closing it behind you, and continue to the right, looking for a windmill on the left. This is Detroit Tank on the U.S. Geological Survey maps. Stop
here and you are in the general area of Paraje San Diego, a most important
location, as you will see.

PARAJE SAN DIEGO

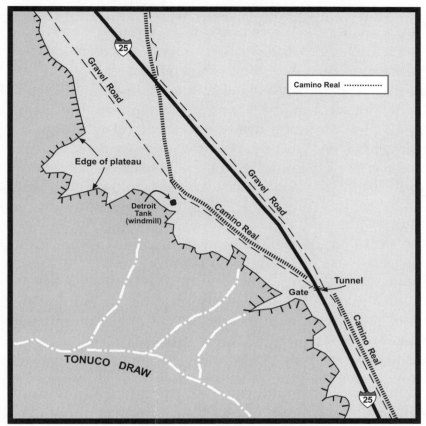

Travelers on the camino needed this paraje as perhaps no other. A glance at the jornada map shows that it was one day's journey from the paraje at Robledo (Fort Selden area). You will also note that this site is perched on the plain peering down on the Rio Grande. Horses, oxen, and mules could be taken from the paraje down Tonuco Draw to be watered. The next day, the caravan would head north toward Fra Cristóbal, two days' journey from here.

The paraje was not a single point but a general area comprising many acres. Travelers wanted to rest somewhere on the "lip" of the plain, which extended for some distance here. Some travelers, in fact, may have gone on to a point closer to today's Rincón. Archaeologists have found evidence of use here from the prehistoric through the nineteenth century. The camino is clearly visible on the east of the gravel road as it heads north.

If you choose the other route from Point of Rocks, the one going to the Upham exit, continue to the interstate, go under it, and take the second road, which heads southeast. (The first road would put you on the interstate.) This road will parallel the interstate. Follow it until you reach the windmill on your right. See the description above for Paraje San Diego.

From Paraje San Diego, return southeast, pass through the gate (again closing it), go under the interstate, and turn right. Take this road (it will pass directly behind the Border Patrol's check station), since it is part of the camino. After going seven miles, you will find a road from the right, which you should take. This will go under the interstate and follow the camino. Continue 1.5 miles until you see a paved road from the left. Take this road to the community of Fort Selden.

Fort Selden

The paved road onto which you have turned becomes Desert Edge Road as you approach Fort Selden. The road bends to your right, away from the interstate, and runs into Tel High Road. Turn left at Tel High and right onto NM 157, also called Fort Selden Road. Descend toward the river until you see the signs for the Fort Selden State Monument. This general area, from the point where you turned onto NM 157 to the river, was Paraje Robledo.

The Robledo paraje was the last paraje for north-bound travelers before entering the Jornada del Muerto. Stopping as they would have done at Paraje San Diego helped shorten the usually waterless stretch north, but Robledo was the last stop on the river, with wood and forage for their livestock. Pedro Robledo, for whom the paraje was named, was a member of Oñate's 1598 caravan who died in this area. The highest peak across the river here, Robledo Mountain, is still named for him.

Fort Selden dates from 1865 and was established, as were Forts Craig and McRae, to protect traders on the camino. It was closed in 1889. The original Camino Real stayed higher than the fort, but after 1865, a branch dipped west to

FORT SELDEN

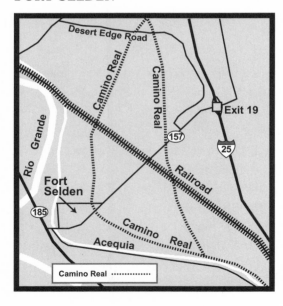

Fort Selden, at the southern end of the jornada, was built in 1865 to protect camino travelers from Apache attacks. Photo by Nicholas Brown. Courtesy of Palace of the Governors, Neg. No.: 1742.

pass through the fort. Douglas MacArthur lived at the fort as a child when his father, Arthur MacArthur, was stationed there. The young MacArthur remembered learning to ride a horse during his stay at Fort Selden.

South of Fort Selden, the precise route of the camino has not been ascertained. This writer feels that the camino followed the valley's east side at the very edge of the floodplain. You saw how the camino followed this pattern between Albuquerque and Bernalillo. The Rio Grande flooded often, so the first dry ground would be just above the flat floodplain. For that matter, the later acequias, or irrigation ditches, probably were dug right on or near the camino.

Thus, if you wish to follow the camino to the next important site, go right after leaving the Fort Selden parking lot, and just after passing the canal, turn left and follow that road (NM 28) as it parallels the irrigation canal. Be careful here as you do not want to go to NM 185. You will pass by Leasburg on the way to the community of Doña Ana. At about one mile past the hamlet of Hill, your road continues adjacent to the railroad tracks, whereas the camino was likely higher up to your left, nearer to the canal.

Doña Ana

At the intersection with NM 320, you will find a marker at the southeast corner, Doña Ana. Doña Ana is to your left, east on NM 320, and should be visited. Doña Ana is first referred to as a paraje. It is likely that this paraje could be any number of locations in the vicinity of the present community of Doña Ana. Certainly by 1846 the community existed, for Wislizenus mentions it as the first town reached south of the jornada.

Note the general rise in elevation as you approach the community and turn right at the first road, Dusty Lane. This road takes you to the small church and plaza area. The town likely had a fortified plaza with connecting houses and one or two gates. This would have been a very dangerous place in the mid-nineteenth century, since it was near both the Mescalero Apaches to the east and the Gila Apaches to the west.

After visiting the town, return to NM 320, turn right, and continue toward the interstate. Immediately before the interstate, turn right onto CR 75, El Camino Real. After about one-half mile, this road actually lies over the camino. Follow it to Las Cruces.

Las Cruces was founded as an American town; that is, after the Mexican War had concluded. A paraje had been in this area, La Ranchería, but few mentioned it. Once again, we can only guess as to the precise route of the camino through Las Cruces. The acequia, which may have followed the camino, is easily found. Water Street in Las Cruces parallels the acequia, just north of it.

When you reach a signal light at North Main, turn right and head for downtown. You will pass sites for two gristmills in town that used falling water from the acequia. The initial Catholic church, St. Genevieve, is long gone, but just off Church Street, on Griggs, a marker identifies the site. Another nearby marker is for the Oñate entrada of 1598.

Continue south on Main Street and angle to the left on Valley Drive to University Avenue and turn left. Notice that University is level until you reach Espina, where it rises slightly, which is almost certainly the route of the camino. Turn right onto Espina and drive through the New Mexico State University campus until you come to Sam Steele Way. Interstate 10 prevents you from following the camino at this point. Go west (right) on Sam Steele to El Paseo Street, cross under the interstate (I-10), and turn immediately left onto Stern Drive to parallel it.

Follow Stern to Tigua Road (Espina on some maps) and turn right into the community of Tortugas. Tortugas was formed concurrently with Las Cruces,

LAS CRUCES

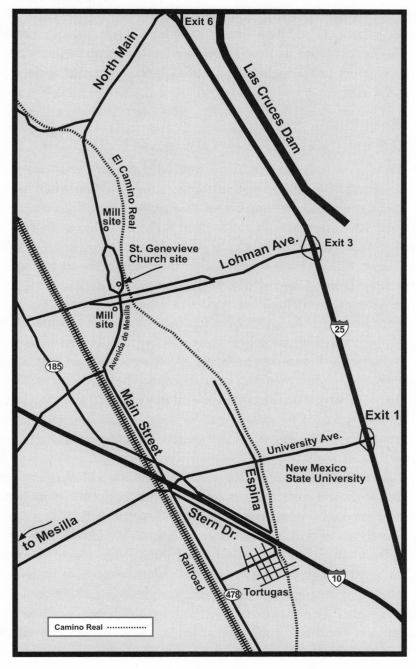

but its residents were Piros, Isletans, or Tompiros from El Paso del Norte. The camino passed directly through the community. Look for Tortugas Drive and turn west on that road, following it to the stoplight at NM 478. Turn left here and go 3.5 miles to Fort Fillmore Road, then turn left there and go past a canal. The fort and cemetery are straight ahead but on private property. You'll have to return to NM 478.

FORT FILLMORE AND THE BATTLE OF BRAZITO

Fort Fillmore, named for President Millard Fillmore, was established in September 1851. The fort played a minor role in the Civil War when in July 1861, thirty-three Confederate troops under the command of Lieutenant Colonel John Baylor moved up the Rio Grande from El Paso. Union forces from the fort met the Confederates across the river at La Mesilla in a minor skirmish (La Mesilla was west of the river in 1861). The Union forces eventually abandoned Fort Fillmore, thinking they were far outnumbered by Confederate forces. In fact, there were far fewer Confederates than Unionists.

After abandoning the fort, Union troops went east up toward San Agustín Pass in the Organ Mountains, where there was a spring. The retreat was a debacle since discipline broke down before the troops reached water and they became easy prey to the pursuing Confederates. They surrendered without a fight. In January 1863, the windows, doors, and wooden frames from the fort's buildings were removed to become part of neighboring houses. Some adobes were also taken, but the walls of the fort melted into the earth during the following years.

Return to NM 478 and turn left again, heading toward El Paso. The camino is toward your left, about where the irrigation canal is today. At two miles, you will see an abandoned schoolhouse, Brazito School, on your left. This is the general area of an early paraje, Los Brazitos. *Brazito* means "little arm" in Spanish, in this case referring to an arm of the Rio Grande, which made a large bend here and came close to the foothills on the east to create a logical stopping place, or paraje.

The battle of Brazito was fought on December 25, 1846, between some five hundred Missourians under Colonel Alexander Doniphan and one thousand Mexicans under Colonel Antonio Ponce de León. National Park Service archaeologists have researched this area extensively, and the accompanying map is based on their findings.

Doniphan's force of about five hundred with no artillery were camped on the camino when they were alerted to a large force of Mexicans coming up the

LAS CRUCES TO EL PASO

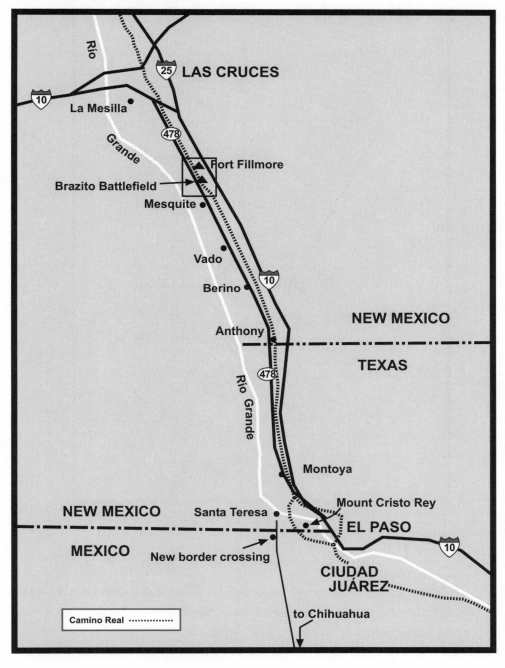

BATTLE OF BRAZITO

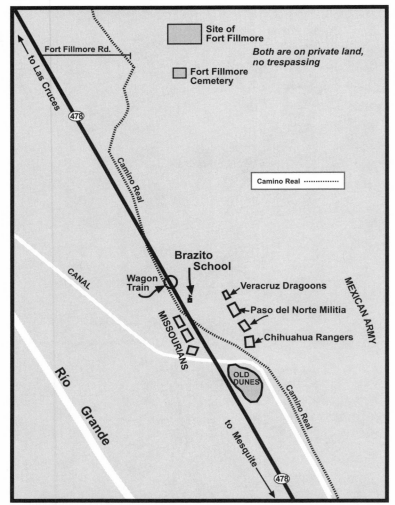

Based on a map by Charles M. Haecker

camino. The ensuing battle lasted less than one hour and ended with the Mexicans in full retreat. They arrived in El Paso in disarray but did not linger there, for they formed part of the army at the later battle at Sacramento. Once you locate the present-day Brazito School building, you will have ample orientation to the battlefield.

Continuing south on US 85/185 from Brazito, you will pass through the small communities of Mesquite, Vado, and Berino. The camino was parallel to

Brazito School south of Las Cruces. The battle between Mexican and American forces in 1846 was fought in this vicinity. Photo by author.

the highway and about halfway between it and the interstate. Again present-day canals are almost on top of the camino. A marker on US 85/185 on the south side, Paraje de los Bracitos, describes the many rest stops near here.

Near Berino was another paraje called Punto del Estero Largo. Several eighteenth-century travelers (Rivera, Lafora) and one seventeenth (Otermín) mentioned this paraje. At Anthony, you pass into Texas. The state line runs through this town. South of Anthony, the Rio Grande will be close on your right. If you have a decent map of this area showing the state line, you should note that it follows the nineteenth-century river channel. When Elephant Butte Dam was completed in 1916, the river was straightened and channeled here.

Look for Vinton, a few miles south of Anthony. Preliminary work by New Mexico State University archaeologists indicates that this may be the site of La Salineta, the paraje used by Otermín when he and two thousand refugees came south in 1680, at the time of the Pueblo Revolt. They camped at La Salineta for several weeks, waiting to move into El Paso del Norte. When excavations are completed, the site may be an important discovery.

ENTRADA TO EL PASO

The Rio Grande valley near present-day El Paso played an important role in the life of the Camino Real and a crucial role for New Mexico. The first Europeans to visit this area were likely the party of Castaño de Sosa in 1590. De Sosa, who had failed in his attempt to colonize New Mexico, passed through the valley with his wagons on his expedition's retreat south.

In 1598 the large caravan of Juan de Oñate entered the Rio Grande valley about forty miles southeast of present-day El Paso. Oñate's "Toma," or ceremony of taking possession, took place on April 30, 1598, on the right bank of the Rio Grande some twenty miles downstream from El Paso. Oñate then continued upstream to "Las Puertas," the place where the river broke through the mountains, providing an important ford of the river. Oñate's ford is near downtown El Paso and Ciudad Juárez.

Oñate's entrada marked the beginning of permanent occupation and settlement by Europeans of the valley. At first only the passage of Franciscan supply trains every two or three years disturbed the area. Soon, however, it became evident to some padres that the ford would make an ideal location for a settlement. Local Manso Indians could be converted to Christianity and supply the labor necessary to build a church and develop an agricultural base. In 1659 construction began on the first mission church, with a more substantial one completed in 1668. This mission was called Nuestra Señora de Guadalupe and is the one we see today in Ciudad Juárez. This nascent community of a few padres and converted Indians, called El Paso del Norte and now Ciudad Juárez, became central to the survival of the entire New Mexico colony.

In 1680 the Pueblo Indians of New Mexico revolted, killing twenty-one of the thirty-three padres, many Christianized Indians, and four hundred settlers. Two thousand survivors, Spanish and Indians, fled south under the command of Governor Otermín. This exodus did not stop until it reached a point on the Rio Grande thirteen miles north of Mission Guadalupe. There Governor Otermín ordered the refugees to pause while he developed a plan for their dispersal into the Rio Grande valley downstream from El Paso del Norte.

El Paso del Norte in 1680 was but a mission church, a few other modest buildings, and a canal bringing water from the river to a few fields. Otermín distributed the refugees in several locations downstream from El Paso del Norte. Each small community had its unique ethnic composition: Piro Indians in one, Tompiro in another, and Indians from Ysleta Pueblo in yet another. Bishop Tamarón, in his inspection tour of 1760, noted these communities and listed the

The cathedral and mission church in Ciudad Juárez. The tower is a nineteenth-century addition to the 1670s church. Photo by the author.

racial composition of each. Little change had taken place in the span of almost a hundred years.

The Pueblo Revolt in New Mexico in 1680 emboldened other Indians to rebel against the Spanish. Local Mansos and Sumas, the Janos southwest of El Paso del Norte, and even Tarahumaras in the Sierra Madre to the west fought the Spanish colonizers with renewed vigor. Presidios had to be established in 1683 in El Paso del Norte, Janos, and San Buenaventura to help defend against these attacks.

Without the small community of Mission Guadalupe, the New Mexico colony would likely have ended in failure in 1680. Otermín and his collection of refugees would have had to continue south to the next Spanish settlement, which in 1680 was at Valle de San Bartolomé, Oñate's starting point in 1598. As it was, the Mission Guadalupe settlement was just well enough established to allow the New Mexicans to regroup and eventually return north to resettle New Mexico in the 1690s under de Vargas.

PLAN OF EL PASO DEL NORTE

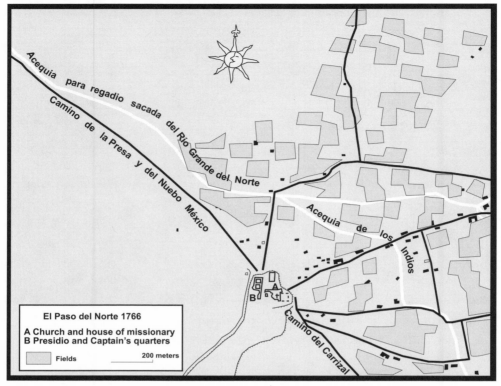

Based on a map drawn by Joseph de Urrutia in 1766

Through the years, El Paso del Norte and its satellite communities of San Lorenzo, Senecú, Ysleta del Sur, and Socorro prospered and grew. When Bishop Tamarón visited the valley in 1760, he counted 4,790 people living in the five communities. The area was already well known for its fine fruits, vegetables, wines, and spirits.

Indian problems persisted in the area, however. The Apaches in particular were troublesome for the valley's residents. After the Spanish crown authorized a study of border defenses in 1765, the Marqués de Rubí was sent in 1766 to inspect the border defenses and ascertain what modifications would strengthen the border against Indian raiders. His report was accepted, and the result was the Reglamento of 1772.

In his report, Rubí suggested that a new "line" should be created, stretching from the Gulf of California to the Gulf of Mexico. This "line" was to have a series of approximately equally spaced presidios (fifteen on the line and two beyond it). Some of the presidios already existed, some were to be built, and some were to be moved. In the case of El Paso del Norte, Rubí felt that the community had sufficient population to be made into militia units so that the presidial soldiers could be moved to Carrizal, a village seventy-five miles south. Carrizal was astride the Camino Real and needed protection from attack by Apaches. The move was accomplished in 1773. Lafora, Rubí's cartographer, proposed a presidio at Robledo, just north of El Paso del Norte, about where Fort Selden came to be built. This presidio, which was to be manned with a few soldiers from Santa Fe, was never built.

The presidio at Guajoquilla, south of Chihuahua on the Río Florido, had earlier been moved to a location almost due east of Carrizal on the Rio Grande. This presidio, renamed San Elceario, was later moved north to a place called Los Tiburcios. Los Tiburcios had been noted by Tamarón in 1760 when he counted the population there as being part of Socorro. Between 1760 and 1780, the Apache attacks at Los Tiburcios had forced the population to abandon it. The new presidio, now called San Elizario, allowed settlers to return to the area. The Texas town of San Elizario is situated at the site of the presidio.

The nineteenth century dawned with Spain still in control of New Spain and still prohibiting its colonies from trade with other countries. The trade with Santa Fe on the camino came increasingly under the control of Chihuahua merchants. Finished products went north on the camino while wool, salt, and other basic products passed south through El Paso del Norte. The pacification policy put in place by Spain in the late eighteenth century seemed to be working. This policy consisted of two parts: the location of the presidios and encouraging the Apaches to settle near presidios to get rations. In 1807 Zebulon Pike passed through El Paso, noting that his host owned twenty thousand sheep and one thousand cows. Prosperity and relative peace with the Apaches could explain this wealth.

Many changes took place in the valley when Mexico gained independence in 1821. Trade was opened to the United States immediately by way of the Santa Fe Trail. Within a few years, goods were flooding through El Paso on their way to Chihuahua, Durango, and even Mexico City. Mexico created the state of Chihuahua in 1824, placing the northern boundary of the state about where Doña Ana, New Mexico, is today. Inspection of trade caravans for proper documentation now took place at El Paso, making it even more important.

The war between Mexico and the United States in 1846–48 led to a decline of the valley's importance. The land north of the river became U.S. territory and part of the state of Texas. Before the war, there had been little activity north of the river. Until 1849 the river followed a course considerably north of where it runs today, so most of the valley lay south of the river. In 1849 a major flood occurred that moved the river south, leaving many miles of the camino in U.S. territory. The Mexican towns of Ysleta del Sur, Socorro, and San Elizario became a part of the United States overnight.

With the river as an international border, trade slowed. Present El Paso, Texas, began as a military outpost (Fort Bliss) and grew in importance. First the California gold rush brought thousands of men through El Paso on their way west. Next the Butterfield stage route was established, connecting St. Louis with San Francisco. As movement shifted from north-south to east-west, the camino withered. Finally, in 1882, a railroad was completed from El Paso to Chihuahua almost on top of the camino. The old road, at least in the north, served only local traffic.

Although this historically important valley is home to approximately 1.5 million residents today, with patience and some caution, many camino sites can be enjoyed. Most are on the Mexican side of the river, but even these are relatively easy to visit.

Lower Crossing

Continue south from Vinton on Texas Highway 20. In Texas this highway is now called Doniphan Drive after Colonel Alexander Doniphan, commander of the U.S. force that invaded here in 1846. His men fought in the Battle of Brazito on December 25, 1846, and afterward he and his forces passed here on their way to El Paso del Norte. After their defeat at Brazito at the hands of Colonel Doniphan, the Mexican army did not pause long at El Paso del Norte but marched south to Chihuahua.

Two miles beyond the intersection with Mesa Street, you will see a road entering from your right at a signal light named Frontera Road. Frontera was another name for the Upper Crossing. Several traders mentioned this crossing in the 1840s, claiming they would cross the Rio Grande here and go west of Mule Driver's Mountain and into El Paso del Norte. Mule Driver's Mountain is today's Mount Cristo Rey, the peak you see to your right front with a cross on top. The actual crossing is unknown since the river has moved, or been moved, to its present location. There is no reason to turn on Frontera.

Continue past Frontera Road to Sunland Park Drive and turn left immediately, looking for direction signs to US 85, Paisano Drive. If you would like to visit Boundary Marker 1, the first marker placed in demarcating the U.S.–Mexico

EL PASO, TEXAS, AND CIUDAD JUÁREZ, MEXICO

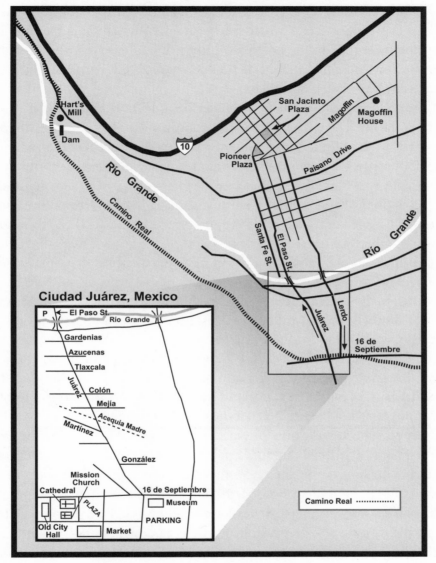

boundary after the Gadsden Purchase, turn right toward Anapra to cross the river. After crossing the river, take the first left on McNutt and continue along the river through a construction area to finally arrive at the marker site. There are markers on both the U.S. and Mexico sides, and Boundary Marker 1 is in a small park open to both nationalities.

Return the way you came to Paisano Drive, then turn right toward El Paso. You are now very close to the Rio Grande, on your right. The camino was just below the modern interstate, which is to your left. After crossing the river, travelers generally looped to the north around the hills. This area was difficult for travelers, with Oñate taking four days to accomplish the seven miles from the river crossing back to the floodplain.

Paisano Drive passes through Smeltertown, with its large copper smelter. This is not the most beautiful part of El Paso. You will note the formidable fence on your right (and you will also see many Border Patrol vehicles) and housing for the poor across the river in Ciudad Juárez. Continue on Paisano until you see a sign for Old Fort Bliss. Turn right here (the fort is now private housing and not open to the public) and continue on this frontage road to a restaurant on the right called La Hacienda Café. Turn into the restaurant's parking lot, where you will see a number of historical markers.

This site is directly above the Lower Crossing, the ford that Oñate used in 1598. The dam for El Paso del Norte's irrigation system is found here as well. Unfortunately, the area has been greatly modified, so that one can't see the crossing or the dam. The dam standing here now provides water for the Mexican side of the river, while water for the United States is taken from the river upstream, near Smeltertown. When Zebulon Pike arrived at this point in 1807, a bridge spanned the river either at this site or a bit upstream. This five-hundred-foot-long bridge was seventeen feet wide and supported by eight caissons. Later travelers did not mention the bridge, so it must have been short-lived.

Markers here include one for Oñate's crossing on May 4, 1598; one for the Camino Real; one for the Franklin Canal; and one of stone for Simeon Hart. In 1847 Hart built a mill at this site across the river from another mill, that of Ponce de León, and he also built a house here in 1854. The restaurant incorporates a portion of his house, making this the oldest building in El Paso. If you walk to the fence on the west side of the parking lot, you look down on the Franklin Canal, the principal diversion for irrigation on the U.S. side of the valley, which more or less followed the Rio Grande before the flood in 1849 changed its course.

Leave the parking lot, turn right, and rejoin US 85 South, Paisano Drive. Follow Paisano to El Paso Street, where you should turn left (it's a one-way street) and go to San Antonio Avenue. Look for parking anywhere in this area. An acequia was dug in the mid-1820s for the farm of Juan María Ponce de León, who had petitioned for a grant of land on the north side of the river. The grant was made on September 25, 1827, and Ponce de León built his first adobe home and then a second home about where the Mills Building now stands, opposite

San Jacinto Plaza. He later sold his holdings to Benjamin Franklin Coons. This area became Coons Ranch and later Franklin. There are several markers in the San Jacinto Plaza, which is at Mills Avenue and San Francisco Avenue.

Magoffin Home

About the only other place of interest downtown is the Magoffin home, at 1120 Magoffin Avenue. To get there, take San Antonio Avenue east to Magoffin Avenue. The left turn onto Magoffin from San Antonio is just past the County Complex at Kansas Avenue. The home, just beyond Octavia Street on your right, is now the Magoffin Home State Park and is open daily from 9 AM to 4 PM. The house was built by Joseph Magoffin, the son of Santa Fe trader James Wiley Magoffin. James Wiley was the brother-in-law of Susan Shelby Magoffin, well known to Santa Fe Trail followers. James Wiley, who was involved in the peaceful transfer of power to the Americans in Santa Fe during General Stephen Watts Kearny's invasion in 1846, married into a prominent Chihuahua family in 1834, which placed him in a good position for the Santa Fe trade. After the war with Mexico, James Wiley Magoffin returned to El Paso del Norte but settled on the Texas side of the river. He ran a trading post in the community that became Magoffinsville, the forerunner of today's El Paso.

James Wiley's son, Joseph, was born in Mexico in 1837 and joined his father in El Paso in 1856. Both Magoffins supported the South during the Civil War, when James Wiley's property was confiscated by federal officials. Joseph managed to regain his father's property and subsequently built this home, beginning in 1873. The home is well worth visiting. It makes a connection between the Santa Fe Trail and the Camino Real and shows how they were related.

After visiting the Magoffin home, you must make a decision. To follow the Camino Real directly (that is, in spatial order), you must cross into Mexico here. You saw the crossing at Simeon Hart's mill site. From the accompanying map, you can see that the Rio Grande's position is very different now than it was during camino times. The river's shift south in 1849 left Ysleta, Socorro, and San Elizario in the United States. That is, before 1849, the camino crossed the river at Hart's Mill and passed through El Paso del Norte, San Lorenzo, Senecú, and then Ysleta del Sur and Socorro. With the shift of the riverbed, the camino now crosses back into the present United States between Senecú and Ysleta.

One other item of interest to us is a new statue being placed at the El Paso International Airport sometime in 2006. This is an equestrian statue some thirty-six feet high, weighing twenty tons. The sculptor is John Houser, and his work here represents Juan de Oñate, but because of local politics, it is named

El Paso del Norte with new and old channels of the Rio Grande

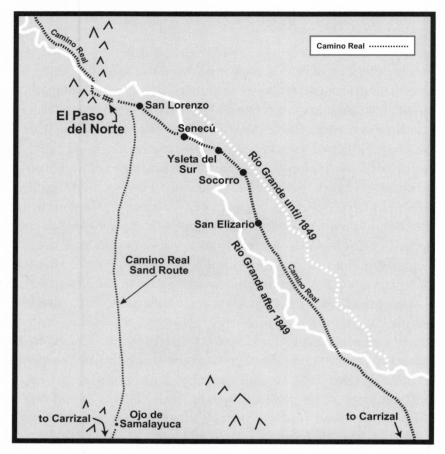

The Equestrian. And it is not just the name of the statue that is the problem but also the location. The statue should be at the Oñate crossing or even in a downtown park, but controversy has relegated it to the airport. This story is related here to remind you of the many perceptions of the Spanish conquest of New Mexico. Oñate is a hero to some, a villain to others.

The best way to view the camino is to cross into Mexico in downtown El Paso on foot. Later, after seeing the old El Paso del Norte sites in downtown Ciudad Juárez, you can return to the U.S. side and drive to other Mexican camino locations south of Ciudad Juárez.

El Paso del Norte (Ciudad Juárez)

Drive back to downtown El Paso from the Magoffin Home and find Santa Fe Street, which is one block west of El Paso Drive. Turn south toward the river and border and drive until you near the border, where you will see many parking lots. A footbridge on your left here passes over the river. Park your car and walk to the footbridge, where you will pay a small fee to cross the river into Mexico (U.S. money is fine). This crossing is also used by cars and is one-way into the United States. Since the waiting time for cars to cross when returning can be very long, it is suggested that you walk. It's only nine short blocks to the plaza from the border.

After crossing into Mexico, you are on Avenida Juárez, named for Benito Juárez, the revered Zapotec Indian who was president of Mexico during the French occupation in the 1860s. This street is typical for border cities, with liquor stores and pharmacies dominating the scene. Although you can change a few dollars into Mexican pesos in several shops along Avenida Juárez, this really isn't necessary, since dollars are accepted everywhere along the border.

When you get to Mejía Street, you should begin to look for clues to the location of the old acequia (see inset on El Paso map, page 85). Both sides of Avenida Juárez, at the point where the old acequia crosses, are lined with small shops. The acequia was covered over here in the 1950s, and the shops came later. This is the "acequia madre," the very one dug in the 1680s and shown on the Urrutia map of 1766. To accomplish their goal of teaching the Indians agriculture, the Spanish padres needed irrigation in this arid climate. The acequia provided them with the necessary water.

Continue on Juárez to 16 de Septiembre, where, on the southeast corner, you will see the 1889 Aduana (Customs House) building. It is now a city museum and well worth a visit. Turning right on 16 de Septiembre, which is the Camino Real here, and walking two blocks will take you to the city plaza, with the cathedral facing it on the west.

Standing next to the cathedral on the left is the modest mission church on which construction was begun about 1659. The early church was improved, but in 1662, the cornerstone was laid for the church you see today. The bell tower is an nineteenth-century addition. The mission church was named Nuestra Señora de Guadalupe for the Mansos Indians. Its founder was Padre García de San Francisco y Zúñiga, who had begun his work in Senecú Pueblo at the north end of the jornada in 1620 but moved south to begin this mission to the Indians.

The Urrutia map, drawn in 1767, shows, in addition to the church, a presidio immediately behind the church. This presidio was built in the 1680s, but the garrison moved in 1773 to Carrizal (seventy-five miles south of El Paso del Norte), since there were enough able-bodied and armed men to protect El Paso del Norte from Apaches. You can also see the acequia madre in Urrutia's map, the same acequia you passed over earlier. Urrutia's map indicates that the church and presidio were built on a bench slightly above the surrounding floodplain. This explains the church's permanence because most early builders in the valley ignored the threat of floods, with the result that their constructions were destroyed. Note the slight rise as you walk along 16 de Septiembre from the museum to the mission church.

After visiting the mission church and cathedral (the cathedral built or rebuilt in 1977 after a fire), you can walk behind the church and view the old city hall, which stands on the site of the eighteenth-century presidio. The camino ran next to the plaza on the river side, on 16 de Septiembre, and headed for the dam and crossing at Hart's Mill. Calle Ugarte is the street that lies on top of the old camino. Ugarte was once known as El Camino de la Presa y del Nuevo Mexico (The Road to the Dam and New Mexico). Urrutia's map shows this camino to the dam, or presa as it is labeled. You might enjoy visiting the public market next to the church as well.

El Paso del Norte began as a religious community when the padres established a mission here in 1659. In 1680 it also became a civilian town with the influx of Pueblo Revolt refugees. The town thrived, growing to forty-eight hundred people as reported by Bishop Tamarón in 1660, to an estimated five thousand by Lafora in 1767, and finally to Wislizenus's estimate of ten thousand to twelve thousand in 1846.

American visitors to the town were almost uniform in their praise. Zebulon Pike in 1807 reported the finely cultivated fields of wheat and numerous vineyards producing "the finest wine ever drunk in the country." Josiah Gregg called it "that delightful town of vineyards and orchards" and its residents "more sober and industrious than those of any other part of Mexico." Wislizenus, in 1846, says of El Paso del Norte that "the houses are surrounded by gardens, orchards, and vineyards." And, he writes, "such scenery may be especially attractive to those recently passing through the jornada." Perhaps this comment explains part of the charm and beauty of El Paso del Norte.

When you return to your car, you are ready to discover other Camino Real communities.

South to San Lorenzo and Senecú

At first Otermín made his headquarters at San Lorenzo de Toma, some thirty miles downriver from Mission Guadalupe. Finally, Otermín brought the settlers to Mission Guadalupe and three camps situated downstream about five

San Lorenzo and Senecú

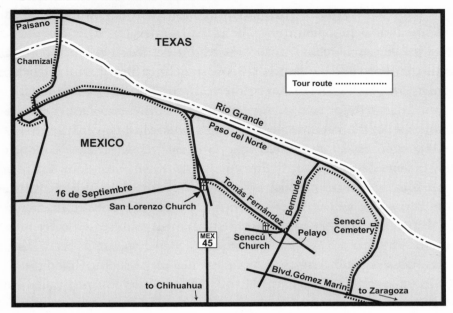

miles apart. Only four years later, a plan was adopted that manifests itself in today's landscape.

First, the community of San Lorenzo de la Toma, which originally had been sited thirty miles downstream, was moved closer to Mission Guadalupe. San Lorenzo (the present one) was home to Suma Indians. A second new community was sited about two leagues (eight miles) beyond San Lorenzo at Senecú, whose name was borrowed from the by then defunct Senecú Pueblo in New Mexico. Piros, Tompiros, and Sumas became the majority population at Senecú.

To get to San Lorenzo and Senecú, drive east on Paisano Drive and take the road heading south toward the Chamizal border crossing. The locals call this the "free bridge." Going into Mexico with your car is an easy entry. Your U.S. car insurance should cover you since you will be only a mile or two from the border at any time, but you should check with your insurance company to confirm this. (See the appendix for suggestions on travel in Mexico.)

Immediately after passing into Mexico, you are in the Chamizal, a contested area not returned to Mexico until the 1960s. Continue straight past Chamizal Park until you pass over another road (about one mile from the border). At the first road past the overpass, turn right, drive a few hundred yards, and turn right once again.

This will place you on Avenida Heroico Militár, a major throughway paralleling the Rio Grande. Continue 1.5 miles to Avenida San Lorenzo (the signs direct you toward the airport, Aeropuerto and Chihuahua) and turn right. At about one mile, you will see the San Lorenzo church looming directly ahead. Park before you get to the church! (If you pass the church, it will be difficult to turn around and head back toward it). Visit the church and bookstore next door. This is, of course, not the original building, but the present church is in the immediate area of the original and is still the center of the San Lorenzo community, dating from the 1680s.

The next 1680s community, Senecú, is located two leagues (about eight miles) beyond San Lorenzo. Before you return to your car, look for the road labeled Tomás Fernández, which is behind (north of) the San Lorenzo church. Tomás Fernández will take you to Senecú. Drive on Tomás Fernández about 2.3 miles to a modern shopping center on your right just before Antonio Bermudez (there is a stoplight at Bermudez). While on Tomás Fernández, you will have passed a golf course on the right and a very tall office building.

On one side of the parking lot, you will see a modest street called Pelayó. Take this unpaved street, which parallels a massive wall on your immediate right, and eventually it becomes paved at Calzada Senecú, where the church will be on your right. Again this is not the original building, and in fact, it may not be close to the original site of the first Senecú church. Bishop Tamarón tells us that Senecú was two leagues from San Lorenzo, and looking at a map will show you that this church is not five miles from San Lorenzo.

Mystery and some controversy surround the location of the Senecú settlement. El Paso, Texas, has a marker claiming the original site was in that city. Recall that the marker site in Texas would have been south of the Rio Grande during the colonial period. Maps from the late nineteenth century show Senecú east of where the church in Mexico is today. Still, we can be certain that Senecú was on the Camino Real and about halfway between San Lorenzo and the next camino community, Ysleta del Sur.

Leaving the Senecú church, retrace your route on Pelayó to Fernández. Turn right on Fernández, then immediately left at the stoplight on Bermudez. Drive on Bermudez to the Viaducto and turn right. The signs you should follow here will say Zaragoza. Continue on the Viaducto until it bends to the right at about 2.5 miles from Dominguez. On your right, about two hundred yards away, you can see a large cemetery. This location is another strong candidate for the 1682 Senecú. Unfortunately, archaeologists have not yet found evidence that this location is that of the original Senecú. The site is nevertheless about halfway between San Lorenzo and Ysleta del Sur, which is where Tamarón placed Senecú.

OÑATE ENTRADA SITE

Continue on the right, or inside, "branch" of the Viaducto to a major intersection. This is México 2, Boulevard Manuel Gómez Marín, which will take you to the next important location. Turn left here and follow the signs toward Zaragoza, but continue past this town toward Guadalupe Bravo. You will become acquainted with *topes*—the little speed bumps used to slow traffic in Mexico. Be careful! It will be thirty-five miles to our next stop, about a forty-five-minute drive and about two hundred topes.

Just before reaching Guadalupe Bravo, you will see signs indicating a border crossing. You will be returning to this spot later and crossing the border here. When you get to Guadalupe Bravo, just past kilometer marker 50, you must turn left at a stop sign on M. Hidalgo to continue on México 2. Three miles past the outer limits of the town, a paved road comes in from the right. There is a commercial sign, Super El Mimbre, here.

Turn toward El Mimbre on this paved road. The little community of El Mimbre is very near the spot where the Camino Real escaped the mountains and entered the Rio Grande valley. The first Spaniard to come through this gap was Juan de Oñate in 1598. After passing here, he continued up the valley on the right bank, pausing only to take possession of New Mexico. This is La Toma, the taking of possession, but its exact location is unknown. We do know it was between here and El Paso del Norte, or more precisely, the crossing at El Paso del Norte.

Although the exact point of entry into the valley is unknown, three possibilities exist. The paraje before entering the valley (that is, the last rest stop before the valley) was at Tinajas de Cantarrecio, which lies on an arroyo south of El Mimbre. The route, then, almost certainly followed this arroyo at least part of the way. The first possibility is that the camino may have come directly toward the river on the road that serves as El Mimbre's main street, the one that has the grocery store (Super El Mimbre). This road, in fact, does continue south and meets up with the road to Cantarrecio eventually. The second possibility is a road that turns into an arroyo some six-tenths mile west of El Mimbre. You can get there by following the acequia that runs just north of town.

The last possibility, and perhaps the strongest candidate, lies just south of the town of Praxedis Guerrero. To get there, return to México 2, turn right, and drive a few miles to the next town. Find the paved road that leaves Guerrero toward the south. Detailed maps even show a named place, San Lorenzo, south of Praxedis Guerrero. Otermín's first headquarters in 1680 were at a place called

Real de San Lorenzo, about six leagues (twenty-four miles) south of El Paso del Norte, "where the road comes into the valley."

Whichever of these places is the correct one, the camino would have continued south to Cantarrecio (singing water), a spot with water that all camino travelers used and many commented upon. This road and location is now on private property and can't be visited. We will pick up this, the principal camino route, south of Ciudad Juárez.

Return to México 2, turn left, and drive to the aforementioned border crossing past Guadalupe Bravo. The sign directs you to Febens, which is Fabens, Texas. Cross into the U.S. at this little-used crossing. After entering Texas, follow the signs directing you to Texas 20. Texas 20 west takes you to Fabens and on toward Clint, where you should turn left at the first stoplight and follow signs to San Elizario. You will begin to see signs saying Mission Trail here, since the Mission Trail group promotes this Texas portion of the Camino Real.

San Elizario

When you reach San Elizario, head for the Presidio Chapel and park. The community here was begun in about 1740 and was called at the time Hacienda de Los Tiburcios. Tamarón had counted its population as part of Socorro in 1760 when he passed through on his inspection tour. This means the community likely had no church of its own at the time. In 1762 the population of Los Tiburcios was over two hundred, including a number of genízaros. (See the sidebar "Genízaros" in Chapter 1.)

When in 1773 the presidial troops of El Paso del Norte were moved to El Carrizal, the situation in Los Tiburcios worsened. Apache attacks drove out most of its residents, and by 1787, it was abandoned. After Rubí's recommendation for a "Line" of presidios was accepted for the most part (see sidebar, page 106-7), the presidial garrison at Guajoquilla was moved, in 1773, to a point forty miles downstream from Los Tiburcios. This location was too remote from Los Tiburcios, however, and the soldiers from Presidio San Elceario, as it was called, could not protect the community of Los Tiburcios. Recognizing their mistake, the Spaniards then moved the presidio to the Tiburcio area and changed its name to San Elizario.

The Spanish border policy now included stationing forces at the line of presidios as well as recognizing that peace could also be obtained by providing the Apaches with rations. The Apaches were more than willing to agglomerate at the many presidio towns where they could collect their rations. In 1793, 63 Apaches lived at San Elizario, with the number increasing to 350 in 1821. Thus

SAN ELIZARIO

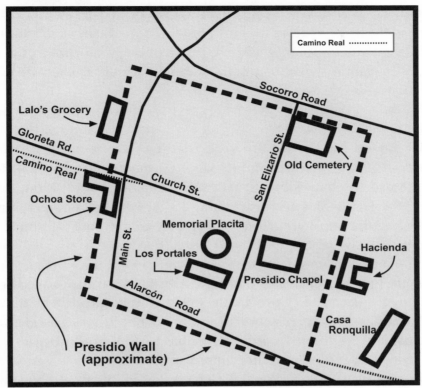

began a period of forty years of relative peace along the border. As you will see, this policy had been used in the Zacatecas region two hundred years before to solve an almost identical problem with intractable Indians.

The accompanying map shows the community of San Elizario as it must have appeared in about 1840. An adobe wall about eighteen feet high and four feet wide was constructed around the presidio. The presidial chapel at that time was probably in the same location as that of the chapel today. Locals recognize that the present chapel, built in 1882, is the fourth building on the same site. The best information about San Elizario can be found at Los Portales, across the street from the chapel. This building, dating from the 1850s, houses the local historical society and a nice museum. Brochures are available here that will direct you on a walking tour of the community.

The accompanying map also shows the location of the presidio walls and a few of the older buildings. One, labeled Hacienda, is simply a house, haciendas being large estates. The Camino Real came into this area from the southeast and left by way of Glorieta Road. One important visitor to San Elizario, Zebulon Pike, noted the many Apaches near the presidio. He said they were "on a treaty with the Spaniards." Susan Magoffin also passed through San Elizario, staying at the house of a family she called Montiz. She said she preferred her tent to staying at homes along the way.

Socorro

From San Elizario, take Glorieta Road, which is the camino, toward El Paso, Texas. In 1.5 miles, Glorieta meets Socorro Road, where you should turn left. Between here and Socorro, you are following the camino. At 10167 Socorro Road, on your right, is Bookery, a bookstore worth visiting. Parts of this building date from the early 1800s. Also, a restaurant called Sombra las Posada on your right dates from about 1852.

You will finally come to the Socorro Mission church on your right. Recently restored, the present church was originally built in 1843. Socorro was one of the communities designated by Governor Otermín in 1680 to be home for the revolt refugees. Suma Indians were assigned to Socorro. Bishop Tamarón listed forty-six families of Sumas at Socorro in 1680 with eighteen families of "citizens," another way of saying non-Indians of perhaps mixed heritage.

The original mission site is near the intersection of Buford Road and Nichols Road, about one-half mile southeast of the present mission church. The original church, built in 1683, was destroyed by one of the many floods to come to the valley. Recall that the Rio Grande at that time flowed between here and the interstate to the northeast.

Ysleta del Sur

From Socorro, continue toward El Paso on Socorro Road on the Mission Trail. In three miles, you come to another Otermín-designated community, Ysleta del Sur. Ysleta is one of only two Indian reservations in Texas and takes great pride in its history and traditions. The Tigua Indian Cultural Center, on the Socorro highway, is well worth a visit. After visiting the cultural center, continue on the highway, then turn right at Old Pueblo Street and circle the plaza to the church.

Ysleta was founded in 1683 at Otermín's direction as a home for Tigua Indians. Many Tiguas had come south in 1680 with Otermín, and he brought almost four hundred additional Isleta Tiguas when he returned in 1682 from his unsuccessful attempt at reconquest of New Mexico. The sister community for Ysleta del Sur is the Isleta Pueblo, just south of Albuquerque.

Church at the pueblo of Ysleta del Sur, near El Paso, Texas. Photo by author.

Today Ysleta del Sur struggles to maintain its Indian traditions and keep good relations with the state of Texas. The Tiguas have had serious differences with Texas over territory and gambling issues. The Tiguas claim much of their land was illegally taken from them. For some years, the Tiguas had a successful casino, the one you see near their church, but the state of Texas closed the casino in 2002. These are but two of the unresolved issues between Texas and the Tiguas.

Built in 1683, the mission church was named Mission Sacramento de los Tiguas de Ysleta. The present church incorporates parts of the original structure.

From Ysleta, head back toward El Paso on Texas 20, which becomes Alameda Avenue. You can also turn left toward the Border Highway, which parallels the river and takes you to the downtown area, or you can turn right on Zaragoza and go to the interstate to achieve the same goal.

CHAPTER FOUR
Chihuahua

The principal Camino Real route leaving El Paso del Norte for the south went through San Lorenzo, Senecú, Ysleta, and Socorro before leaving the valley and heading for Cantarrecio. A secondary route, although shorter by far, passed through the *médanos*, the sand dunes. These dunes form an east-to-west barrier that made it almost impossible for loaded wagons to traverse them. Oñate, coming from the south in 1598, was forced to turn east and go through Cantarrecio when he came to these dunes.

Not that going down the river and passing through Cantarrecio was an easy task. Travelers considered there to be three jornadas between Santa Fe and Chihuahua. The first, the Jornada del Muerto, we visited earlier in New Mexico. The second was this one through Cantarrecio, and it could be a problem. (The third jornada was south of the Río Carmen and was the least troublesome.) Water was generally found at Cantarrecio, but beyond there, travelers hoped that water could be found at Charco el Grado, a sporadically flowing spring about halfway between Cantarrecio and Ojo Lucero, the next stop at about the junction of the "sand" route and the Cantarrecio route.

At Ojo Lucero, travelers would be close to the Río Carmen and Laguna de los Patos, two dependable water sources. The presence of water had brought settlers to this valley in the early 1700s, when Hacienda Carrizal was founded. Using the distant Ojo de Carrizal, the hacienda raised crops and livestock. Other haciendas followed, but all had to be abandoned in the mid-1700s because of Apache depredations. Carrizal itself became a presidio and town in 1773.

The camino route south from Carrizal was very flat and had but one short jornada before reaching Ojo Gallego. From the ojo south, the camino travelers had ready access to water. Near Laguna Encinillas, another large hacienda was established in the early 1700s that was able to resist Indian attacks. Virtually every traveler mentioned Hacienda de Encinillas.

This route also ran directly through the battleground at the Río Sacramento, where in 1847, Colonel Doniphan and his Missouri volunteers met a large Mexican army on the Camino Real nearby. After defeating the Mexican army here, Doniphan's forces marched into the city of Chihuahua unopposed, an important victory that clearly decided the outcome of the war in the Southwest.

Twenty miles beyond the battlefield is the capital of the state of Chihuahua, Chihuahua city. Chihuahua was sited in 1709 to support the silver-mining community of Santa Eulalia, fifteen miles distant. By 1847, and Doniphan's occupation, the city had come to dominate trade and commerce in north-central Mexico. It was far larger than either Santa Fe or El Paso del Norte as well as being a truly urban place with stone church, aqueduct, and permanent buildings around its plaza. The section of the Camino Real from El Paso to Chihuahua is very interesting and steeped in trail lore.

Now that you are ready to begin following the Camino Real toward Chihuahua, you are reminded that you will need a tourist card, car permit, and Mexican auto insurance to drive beyond the customs checkpoint south of Ciudad Juárez. What you will need and how to get these permits is found in the appendix.

A simple way to head south from El Paso is to return to the "free bridge" and drive south following the signs to the *aeropuerto* and Chihuahua. This is the same bridge and route you used to get to San Lorenzo earlier. This time, however, when you approach San Lorenzo, continue south past the church. Mexican highway 45 will take you to Chihuahua, Durango, Zacatecas, and eventually Mexico City.

Another, even easier way is to utilize the new border crossing from Santa Teresa, New Mexico. To do so, take Interstate 10 north past El Paso and look for the sign to Santa Teresa at Exit 8. This road takes you to the new crossing, where Mexican authorities have recently allowed tourists to get their travel documents and thus avoid the drive through Ciudad Juárez. After obtaining your documents, continue south. The road becomes a toll road, to meet with México 45, where you turn right toward Chihuahua.

Ciudad Juárez to Samalayuca

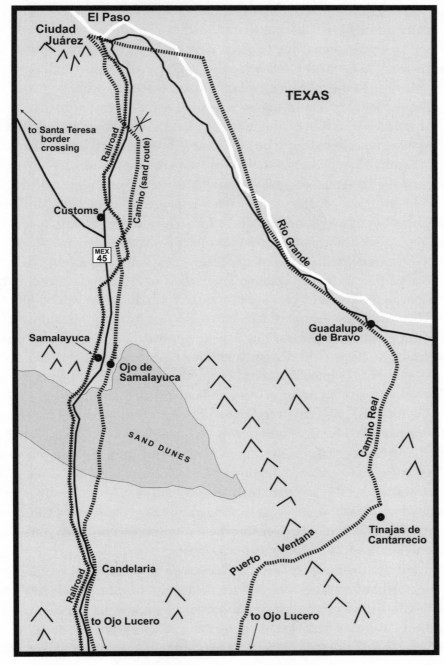

El Paso

Ciudad Juárez

to Santa Teresa border crossing

TEXAS

Railroad

Camino (sand route)

Customs

MEX 45

Río Grande

Guadalupe de Bravo

Samalayuca

Ojo de Samalayuca

Camino Real

SAND DUNES

Tinajas de Cantarrecio

Candelaria

Puerto Ventana

Railroad

to Ojo Lucero

to Ojo Lucero

SAMALAYUCA

After passing through customs south of Ciudad Juárez (this will take more than one hour), you will soon come to signs directing you to Samalayuca. From Ciudad Juárez, you have been following the "sand route" of the camino, which takes you directly to the médanos, or sand dunes, especially visible on your left toward the mountains. These dunes presented a major east-west barrier to camino travelers. Since those using wagons found it was almost impossible to come this way, they chose the route along the Rio Grande. We'll meet up with that route south of Samalayuca. Josiah Gregg wrote that as "teams are never able to haul the loaded wagons over this region of loose sand, we engaged an atajo of mules at El Paso, upon which to convey our goods across." In fact, this route was used almost solely by atajos, mule trains, with wagons utilizing the longer route that you saw earlier entering the river valley near Guadalupe Bravo.

Leave the four-lane highway to take the road to Samalayuca. In this village, you will see your first Ruta de Oñate marker, on your right in the center of the village. Dozens of these markers are in the state of Chihuahua along Oñate's route, each with a quote from Villagrá, Oñate's poetic travel companion. About halfway through town, at a sign saying *retorno* (return), take the road to the east, left, that leads you back to the divided highway. When you arrive at the highway, you can see a road across the highway, beyond the northbound lanes, that leads to Ojo de Samalayuca. A cluster of trees in the distance tells you where the ojo, or spring, is located. This was a very important spring at the edge of the dunes. Unfortunately, the ojo is being "developed," and access is no longer permitted.

The ojo at Samalayuca elicited different responses from travelers who used it. Gregg, for example, called it a fetid pool. Ruxton similarly called it a dirty, stagnant pool, while Pike, stopping there in 1807, said simply that it was a "small pond made by a spring which arose in the center, called Ogo mall a Ukap, and seemed formed by providence to enable the human race to pass that route, as it was the only water within sixty miles on the route."

Turn right at the highway and continue south a few hundred yards. To the east of the northbound lanes, you will see a dirt road leading east. If you wish, you can take that road a short distance and view the route of the trail here. To do this, continue south past marker 317 and make a U-turn, taking you north on the highway. The dirt road is marked by two concrete posts, one on each side. Turn here and park your car soon because the sand is loose. A short walk east will take you to an arroyo that leads south on the camino. Since it was principally used by mules and horses, it lacks the broad swale you might expect.

A *Ruta de Oñate marker
at Samalayuca, south
of Ciudad Juárez. The
comments are by Villagrá,
a member of the Oñate
party. These markers will
be seen through much
of the Chihuahua state.
Photo by author.*

Nevertheless, the route is discernible, climbing up to the narrow pass to the south. If you have made the walk described above, then you must drive north until you can make another U-turn and then continue south on the divided highway through the dunes. It you look carefully at this landscape, you will see a very thin covering of shrub on top of the sand, an almost-impossible situation for heavily laden wagons. At about ten kilometers (six miles) south of the dunes, you should look for a sign, Candelaria, at about KM marker 291. This is about where Oñate turned east to avoid the dunes.

As you continue south, you will note a prominent flat-topped mountain to your right front (at about KM 270). The author, because of its prominence and proximity to Ojo Lucero, calls it Lucero Peak (Sierra San Miguel on Mexican maps), and it tells you that you are approaching Ojo Lucero. This ojo, noted by all nineteenth-century American travelers, marked the first dependable water source south of the dunes, at the approximate junction between the sand and Cantarrecio routes. The camino crosses the highway between KM markers 263 and 262. These markers will be seen soon after the highway passes over the railroad. To find the crossing, look for a yellow post on the west side and an orange post on the east side. Park your car and look for the trace of the camino. To the east of the highway is the railbed, with the camino heading in a northeast direction toward Charcos de Grado, another spring, and then to Cantarrecio. On the west of the highway, you can also detect the camino as it led toward Ojo Lucero and on to Carrizal. Continue south on México 45 to KM 261, where you will see a Ruta Oñate marker on your left. Some buildings in disrepair stand behind the marker on the site of the long-abandoned Lucero train station. The earliest automobile route also came in here from Cantarrecio and the Rio Grande.

OJO LUCERO

The ojo is now an *alberca*, a reservoir and swimming pool, just off the highway to the west near KM marker 259. Turn right here and drive to the alberca. Today this ojo would be dried up if it weren't for wells that pump water to the surface. The many wells in the valley have dried up all the natural ojos, or springs. In the Lucero site, you can see that the well water is pumped into a reservoir that approximates the older ojo.

From Ojo Lucero, continue south on the divided highway toward Villa Ahumada. At KM marker 253, on the left, you can see what remains of Laguna de los Patos. This lake, which even in trail days fluctuated greatly in size, gets its water from the Río del Carmen, an intermittent stream flowing from the south. You will cross this river several times as you progress south and will likely wonder how it could have ever had water in it. But summer rains can easily fill the river to overflowing in a matter of minutes. Many travelers wrote that they had to wait for its water to recede before passing.

Past Laguna de los Patos, you will enter the only real town between Ciudad Juárez and Chihuahua. Villa Ahumada has several motels and restaurants as well as an ATM machine (east of the tracks at a bank near the train station) to replenish your supply of pesos. The town is a good resting spot for modern camino travelers. For a listing of motels and restaurants, see the appendix. There is also a Ruta de Oñate marker near the train station just east of the tracks.

From Villa Ahumada, you can drive west and visit the old community and presidio of Carrizal. To get to Carrizal, properly San Fernando de Carrizal, turn

Ojo Lucero and Carrizal

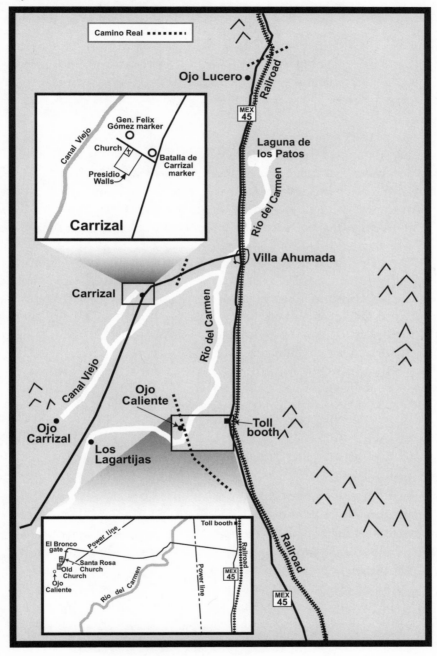

The Line

Protection of the settlers of the northern provinces had always been a major challenge for the Spanish. Not only were they not very successful at protection but their failing strategies were costing the crown considerable sums. Any plan to improve protection, especially if the plan also saved the crown money, was welcomed.

Brigadier Pedro de Rivera was sent north from Mexico City in 1724 on an inspection tour of frontier defenses. It took Rivera more than three years to complete his tour (it included New Mexico, Sonora, and Texas) and write his recommendations, which were mostly accepted by the crown and became the Reglamento of 1729. This *reglamento* was directed more toward cutting costs than improving defenses. It reduced the number of troops and set a pay scale for the soldiers.

The crown, recognizing the changing geopolitical map after the Paris Treaty of 1763 (France ceded all its lands west of the Mississippi River to Spain), sought again to improve the defense of the frontier. The enemy, in the north, anyway, was the Apaches. Between 1749 and 1763, Apaches killed more than eight hundred citizens and destroyed four million pesos of property within a few hundred miles of Chihuahua.

Another inspection was ordered, this one under the command of the Marqués de Rubí. His skilled assistants were Captain Nicolás de Lafora and Sublieutenant José Urrutia. You have seen two of Urrutia's maps in previous sections, and two more will appear later. Rubí's company left Mexico City in March 1766 and returned, after a seventy-five-hundred-mile journey, in February 1768. His recommendations were accepted and resulted in the Reglamento of 1772.

Rubí's most important conclusion was that Spain should limit its control of claimed regions to those areas that were effectively occupied by citizens. This meant that in Texas, many presidios were closed and their garrisons moved south. For the western frontier, it meant moving some garrisons to new presidios in more effective locations.

The accompanying map shows the movement of presidios in the western region. The presidio garrison at Guajoquilla was first moved to a point on the Rio Grande east of Carrizal, which proved to be too far from the line of communities in the El Paso del Norte area, so it was then moved a second time to San Elizario (note change of spelling), which you visited in Texas. As a result, a line of presidios, Rubí called it the Line, stretched from Sonora

The line of presidios as proposed by Marqués de Rubí

through New Mexico and on into Texas. Only two presidios were allowed to remain north of the Line: Santa Fe in New Mexico and San Antonio de Bexar in Texas.

Was this new Line plan a success? Not really. Like the earlier plan, it saved the crown some money but didn't protect the settlers any better. For that matter, from 1771–6, the garrison troops spent most of their time constructing the new presidios, leaving less time to seek out the enemy Apaches. The Line plan resulted in fifteen presidios on the Line plus the two (Santa Fe and San Antonio) beyond it, with seven closed. Still, relative peace came in the last decade of the eighteenth century, when the Apaches were encouraged to gather at presidios and given rations if they remained there. This is the same plan that had worked well in the troubled region around Zacatecas in the sixteenth century.

Note that the map shows a proposed presidio at Robledo. This smaller fort was to be garrisoned with troops from Santa Fe. Robledo was never built, but the importance of that site was later recognized by the Americans, who built Fort Selden there.

west in Villa Ahumada toward Ricardo Flores Magón on Chihuahua 7. As you leave town, you cross the Río del Carmen, but it is usually dry. Continue west to KM 7, where you see a road to your right. Take this road one-half mile and look for the trace of the camino on your left. It will consist of a broad swath of dry grass much different than its surroundings. This is the continuation of the camino you saw near Ojo Lucero that from here passes by Carrizal and on to Ojo Caliente, a later stop on your route.

CARRIZAL

Return to the highway, turn right, and follow the road until you come to Carrizal at KM marker 15. Turn right at a large marker, Batalla de Carrizal, on your right, and you should turn right here, drive to the church, and park your car. Carrizal, or San Fernando las Amarillas del Carrizal, was first sited in the early 1700s as an agricultural and ranching settlement that was watered by a twenty-five-kilometer-long acequia from Ojo Carrizal to the west. It finally succumbed to attacks by Apaches and by the 1770s was abandoned. Bishop Tamarón, on his 1760 inspection tour, noted 41 families with 171 persons living here. At this time, Carrizal was the southernmost community in Nuevo México.

We can get a sense of Carrizal's early history by reading the journals of two early visitors. Pedro de Rivera wrote that in May 1726, while camping at nearby Ojo Caliente, he was visited by a group of Suma Indians from the paraje at Carrizal. They were apparently the only residents at the time. Nicolás de Lafora, Rubí's assistant, who was there in July 1767, tells us more about Carrizal. He reported, erroneously, that it was founded "seven years ago." At the time of his visit, the Apaches were a constant threat, so much so that a squad of ten men and a corporal were assigned here from the presidio at El Paso del Norte. Lafora wrote that most of the men's time was spent caring for their horses, so they were of little use in protecting settlers.

Lieutenant Colonel Hugo O'Conor, fulfilling the directives of the Reglamento of 1772, moved a garrison here from the presidio at El Paso del Norte in 1773 and directed that a new presidio be constructed. About seventy-three soldiers were stationed here in the late 1700s. This presidio was noted by all American chroniclers, including Gregg, Wislizenus, and Magoffin. Although not precisely on the Camino Real, the community was noted by most travelers who regularly visited it.

The present church is modified somewhat from its presidio days (see drawing for comparison). The presidio and its walls have long since melted into the earth, with only some mounds to indicate where its walls were. The walls were

These mounds are all that remains of the presidio walls at Carrizal. The accompanying map of the presidio will allow you to find the mounds of the diamond-shaped tower. Photo by author.

likely ten feet high and four feet thick, with two gates allowing entrance. A corral was in back. As you walk around the site today, you can see the mounds where the walls stood, even the larger mound with its diamond-shaped tower in the south corner. Josiah Gregg placed three hundred to four hundred residents in Carrizal when he passed through in the 1830s. Today only a few families reside here, and they do not farm the old fields of Carrizal because its acequia is now dry. One resident said that if they want water in the acequia today, they pay a rancher upstream to pump groundwater into it.

In front of the church is a striking monument to General Felix U. Gómez and the Mexican heroes of the Battle of Carrizal. During the American intervention following Pancho Villa's attack on Columbus, New Mexico, two companies of American Buffalo Soldiers passed through the area in June 1916, searching for Pancho Villa. As they tried to enter Carrizal, they were warned by General Gómez (his forces were not a part of Villa's but were regular Mexican Army) not to pass

PLAN OF CARRIZAL PRESIDIO, BASED ON A SKETCH BY REX GERALD

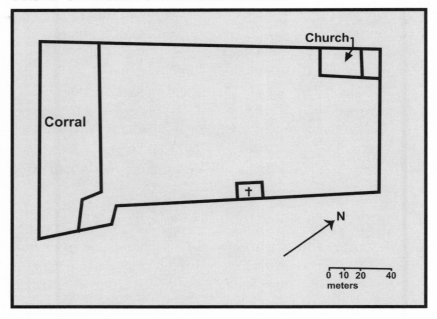

through Carrizal but to go around. The American commanders ignored the warning and were attacked when they marched into town. Some Americans were killed, others captured, but it was a Mexican victory and is remembered today.

The Río del Carmen, although near Carrizal, did not provide the water for its acequia. A canal, twenty-five kilometers in length, brought water to the town. To reach the ojo, or source, for the acequia, turn right on México 7 after leaving Carrizal. At about KM marker 37, or fifteen miles from Carrizal, a road to the right will take you to Ojo de Carrizal.

From the highway, it is 3.3 miles to the ojo. The only evidence of the now dried-up spring is two dead cottonwood trees. You should park nearby and walk to the ojo, continuing down the old canal. This area was first settled in the seventeenth century.

When you return to México 7, you can also cross the highway and drive a short distance to a small community called Lagartija. You will cross over the Río del Carmen just before reaching Lagartija, which apparently began life as a hacienda. Apache attacks led to its abandonment in the mid-eighteenth century. Return to Villa Ahumada on México 7.

OJO CALIENTE

In Villa Ahumada, turn right on México 45 toward Chihuahua. At KM marker 218, you will arrive at your first toll booth. Just past the booth, you'll see a road to your right toward La Rosita, just before KM 216. This road is opposite a collection of ruined buildings that once were the train station Ojo Caliente. (A caution here. If there have been recent rains, postpone your visit.) This road takes you to Ojo Caliente, a well-known stop on the Camino Real (see inset map of Ojo Caliente). Continue west but always veering to the left. You'll come to a corral on your left, which will tell you that you are on the right road. You will cross once again the Río del Carmen and finally arrive at a T in the road. You should look for a stone church off to your left front as you drive west, since this church is very near Ojo Caliente. The junction is unmarked but is called El Bronco. Look carefully to your left and you will see a trace going south toward the stone church. In a few hundred yards, you will come to a cattle gate. Go through it, closing it behind you. You will be approaching the reddish-colored stone church, Santa Rosa. Continue past the church until the road degenerates, then park. From here a short walk leads to Ojo Caliente.

Most nineteenth-century travelers mention this important spring. Adolph Wislizenus even tells us that its waters were eighty-two degrees Fahrenheit. Thus the name *caliente*, or "hot" in English. The site was originally settled in the early seventeenth century and used more or less continually until the twentieth century. When you approach it, you will first see an abandoned adobe church with cemetery. Beyond this church one hundred yards is the actual ojo. Dry now, it was originally filled with warm water from the spring at the base of the hill to your right. On the back side of the opening, you can discern the remains of an eighteenth-century wall that probably encircled the spring at one time. After viewing the ojo, church, and cemetery, look for the camino. You will find it as a broad swath behind the church. From here the camino led north to Carrizal and Ojo Lucero.

Susan Magoffin, who stayed at Ojo Caliente for several days in 1847, says the "Ojo Caliente is a pretty place; the water bursts out at the foot of a hill making a beautiful pool, which is some four or five feet deep, perfectly clear, and warm." Gregg thought that if the spring were in the United States, it would be made into a fashionable resort.

Return to the main highway and turn south. From this point, the camino will be principally on your left as you drive toward Chihuahua. At KM 155, at the small community of El Sueco, turn off the highway and pass through the scattered

The famous Ojo Caliente, now dried up. A small portion of a wall is seen in back, which may date from the 1720s, when there was a hacienda here. Photo by author.

houses to the southeast. Ojo Gallego, a noted stop for caravans, is situated in a canyon to the east, in the Sierra Gallego. You will reach a cattle gate, which you can go through (close it after you), and head east toward the arroyo ahead. Ojo Gallego is found in that canyon but is now dry. The Camino Real can be detected just east of the gate you entered. El Sueco is at a highway junction where you will see another Oñate marker on the east side, near the gasoline station.

Return to the highway, then turn left, heading south again toward Chihuahua. At KM 138, you reach the "summit" of the camino in Chihuahua—this is the highest elevation (5,495 feet) it reaches. Between KM markers 125 and 124 a road to the left (east) heads toward La Esperanza. Turn here and drive a few hundred feet past the electrical station on the left. Immediately beyond the station, you can see the camino coming in from the north. From here it will cross the highway as it drops into the valley of Encinillas.

About where you cross the railroad tracks, the camino has passed to your right, then almost at the crossing, it passes over to the left again, where it will remain all the way to Chihuahua. From here south, the railroad track is a close approximation of the Camino Real. The next camino site is the Hacienda Encinillas, a few miles south of Laguna de Encinillas, a large lake, or lake bed, on your left. It is generally dry. The hacienda lies to the southwest of the camino and south of the laguna. Settled in the late seventeenth century, it is mentioned by many travelers stopping here. Gregg says that the valley was "the locale of one of those princely estates which are so abundant further south, and known by the name of *Haciendas*." On one trip, Gregg ran afoul of the *hacendado* (owner) of the hacienda, Angel Trías, when Gregg shot a cow for food, intending, so he says, to pay for it later. Gregg was eventually ordered to return to Chihuahua to settle the affair.

Beyond Encinillas, the next site is at El Sauz, where a road intersecting México 45 will take you to this modest-size community. Continuing north, on the east side of the railroad tracks, you will reach the deserted community of El Peñol, another location on the camino. Apparently a hacienda stood here, again owned by Angel Trías, that many travelers stopped at, but no remains of the hacienda are seen today, only a few deserted buildings.

BATTLE OF SACRAMENTO

After you pay the toll at the booth on México 45, look for the large white obelisk to your left. Drive to the obelisk, where there is parking. Looking at the included maps, you will discover where you are with respect to the Battle of Sacramento, which was fought here. Look on the map for Mexicans' Second Position. The obelisk stands about where you see the *P* in *Position* on the map. Doniphan arrived at this point with one thousand troops and a few artillery pieces to be met by a Mexican force of four thousand under General José Heredia. The battle did not last very long but, it had far-reaching import for the American Southwest.

The obelisk stands just a few hundred feet west of where the Camino Real passed. The Mexican artillery were situated so they could fire on the Americans as they followed the camino up out of Arroyo Seco, but Doniphan's force had veered to its right before crossing the arroyo. Doniphan, by moving to his right, denied much of the Mexicans' advantage. Once the American forces gained the elevation of the plateau, they attacked the Mexican forces with artillery, cavalry, and infantry.

The battle lasted only three hours. Of the four thousand Mexicans, some three hundred were killed. Doniphan's force, on the other hand, was just over

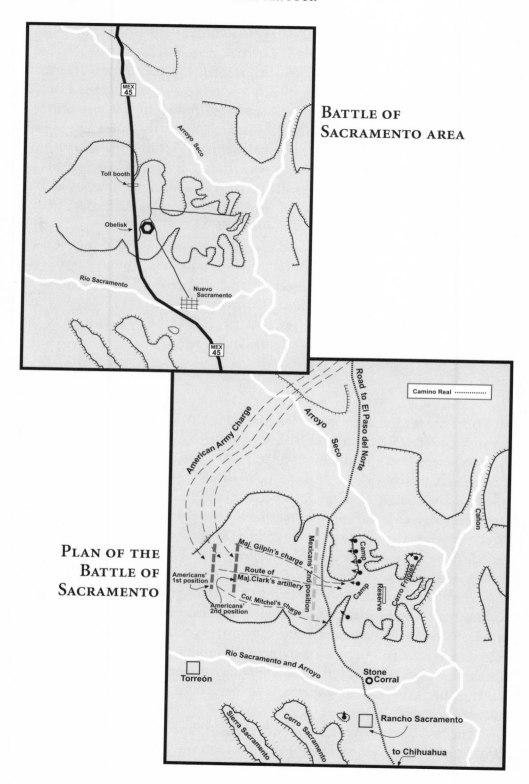

BATTLE OF SACRAMENTO AREA

PLAN OF THE BATTLE OF SACRAMENTO

A lunette for Mexican artillery at the Sacramento.
It is situated overlooking the Arroyo Seco on the north side
of the battlefield. Photo by author.

900 men plus a corps of merchants and teamsters numbering 150 men, commanded by Samuel Owens, a Santa Fe trader of long standing. Of these, Owens was the only American killed in the battle.

To see the camino and placement of the Mexican artillery, take the road behind the obelisk and head left, north. As you drive on the road, look to your right in the arroyo and look for the swales of the camino. Turn right just before the entrance to a gated community. Go east over the arroyo for about one-half mile and turn left. Follow this road down the east side of the arroyo and park somewhere near the barbed wire fence. Walk to the edge of the arroyo, where, looking north, you can see the Arroyo Seco with the camino dropping into it. The edge you are standing on is about where the Mexican artillery was situated. One battery is still there, about two hundred yards to the east of the arroyo, in an area called Cerro Frijoles on one contemporary map.

CHIHUAHUA CITY

After visiting the battlefield, return to México 45 and drive toward Chihuahua. The state capital, Chihuahua is a medium-size Mexican city of about six hundred thousand residents. The simplest way to arrange your visit to the city is to first head for your lodging (see the appendix for a suggestion). Once you get there, the hotel will likely have maps and brochures that will help you orient yourself for your explorations.

Chihuahua, founded on October 12, 1709, as Real de San Francisco de Cuellar, was made a villa (town) in 1718 with the new name San Felipe El Real de Chihuahua. Finally, in 1824, it was designated capital of the new Mexican state of Chihuahua with the simple name Chihuahua. Sited at the confluence of the Ríos Chuviscar and Sacramento, this area was chosen to serve the nearby mines at Santa Eulalia (now Aquiles Serdan). It was not possible to have a city of any size at the mines themselves because of difficult terrain and lack of water. Actually, the Spanish first settled in this area at Nombre de Dios on the Río Sacramento in 1697, where a mission church was built to serve the local Conchos and Chinarras Indian population. Nombre de Dios is now part of the city of Chihuahua. Oñate entered the Chihuahua area on March 12, 1598, at a river they named Nombre de Dios (the Río Chuviscar today). Oñate's friars also named the river that came from the north the Río Sacramento.

When Lafora visited this area in 1766, he counted "four hundred families of Spaniards, mestizos, and mulattoes, who are perishing because of the total failure of the mines." He said the failure here was also a result of Indian attacks and the theft of the horses and mules. Besides the Indian pueblo of Nombre de Dios, he mentioned the church of Nuestra Señora de Guadalupe, which served some thirty Yaqui Indians. These Indians from the Sonora area could only have been brought here to work in the mines.

The downtown area (see map) has a fine cathedral (A), which was begun in 1727, consecrated in 1795, but not completely finished until 1826. One of Mexico's best Mexican examples of baroque architecture, it is situated on a typical and attractive plaza, Plaza de Armas. Unfortunately, the cathedral is the only building on the plaza of any age. The other buildings are all postcamino. During the period 1825–47, the plaza area was filled with commercial buildings used mainly for the camino traffic. Many ventures were foreign controlled: British, French, and American. Goods were brought here from Santa Fé, Mexico City, Vera Cruz, and Mazatlán and were shipped on to other towns and mining communities.

CHIHUAHUA

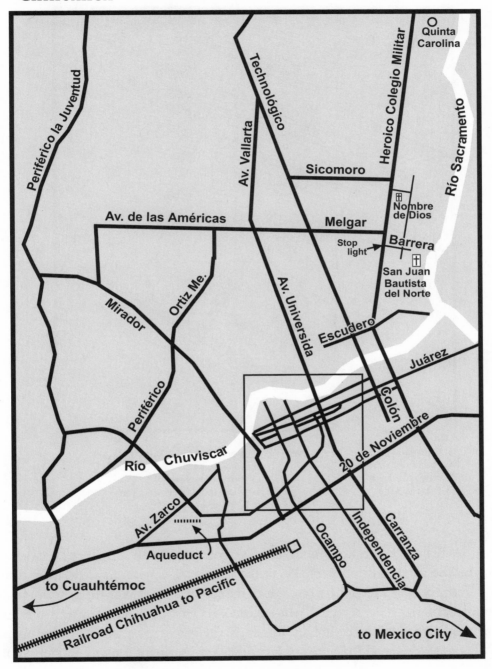

Downtown Chihuahua

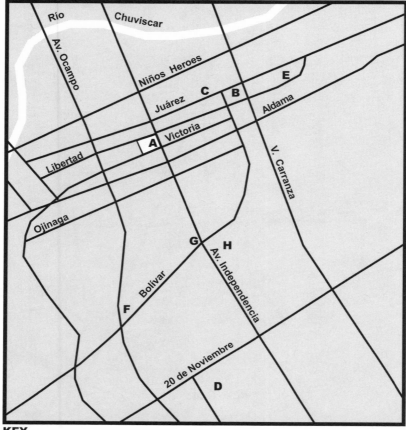

KEY

A Cathedral and Plaza de Armas
B Hidalgo's Dungeon
C Museo Juárez
D Pancho Villa

E San Francisco Church
F Parque Lerdo
G First Cemetery
H Parque de la Revolución

When George F. Ruxton visited the city in 1847, he made several comments about the plaza and cathedral. He noted that at the time of his visit, there were "over the portals which form one side of the square . . . dangling the grim scalps of one hundred seventy Apaches, who had lately been most treacherously and inhumanely butchered by the Indian hunters in the pay of the state." At the time, the Mexicans were paying a bounty of fifty dollars per scalp for Indians. Ruxton mentions the most notorious of the scalp hunters, James Kirker, an Irishman. The Mexicans stopped paying bounties for scalps in part because they discovered that Kirker and others were scalping Mexicans as well as Indians to collect the prizes.

W. H. Jackson took this photo of the Chihuahua cathedral and plaza in the 1880s. Photo courtesy of the Palace of the Governors, Neg. No.: 74696.

On the west side of the cathedral runs Calle Libertad, and one block farther on is Avenida Juárez, which was the Camino Real through the city center. The camino continued west on Juárez, turning south on Avenida Ocampo. From there, it continued south to Paseo Bolívar, which is where Parque Lerdo (F) is situated today. It was called Alameda Santa Rita, and at its south side was the terminal where travelers left the city for the south. Going east, at Bolívar and Avenida Independencia, you will find a park situated on what was the first city cemetery (G). In 1811 the executed leaders of the revolution for independence were buried here, most prominent among them Miguel Hidalgo y Costilla,

Don Santiago Kirker

There is no better way to bring to life the turmoil in Chihuahua and New Mexico in the period after 1830 than to describe the life of James Kirker. Kirker was born in Ireland in 1793, migrated to the United States to escape the British draft in 1810, fought in the War of 1812, then moved west in 1817 to St. Louis, where he worked for the firm of McKnight and Brady.

In 1824 we find Kirker in the Santa Fe trade. He must have been a part-time trader, since he also trapped in the Rockies and along the Gila River. Kirker worked at the Santa Rita copper mine for Robert McKnight for a while. He married a Mexican woman in 1833 (he had left a wife and son in New York), then acquired Mexican citizenship and began trading with the Apaches. This latter activity brought him trouble with the Mexican authorities.

By 1840 Kirker had contracted with the governor of Chihuahua to seek out and kill Apaches, with the hope of exterminating them. Sometimes Kirker received fifty dollars per scalp, other times he worked for one dollar per day. Either way, the Chihuahua governor couldn't afford Kirker, since he brought hundreds of scalps to Chihuahua for the bounty. In an 1847 interview, Kirker claimed that he and his men killed more than 450 Apaches. Many of the scalps were paid for by the Mexican government in Chihuahua. Ruxton, in 1846, was witness to over one hundred scalps hanging from plaza *portales* across from the church in Chihuahua.

Santiago Kirker (sometimes the last name was spelled Querquer), the version of his name the Mexicans used, gave up scalping Apaches for service in Doniphan's army in 1847. John Taylor Hughes, a soldier in Doniphan's service, called him Captain James Kirker and said he left his family to join his countrymen in the army. Since he was a Mexican citizen, one must ask who his countrymen were. Kirker served as scout for Doniphan, succeeding so well that he was cited for his service. He went on to California, where he died in 1853.

Apaches (and more so Comanches) were a thorn in the side of Mexico after 1830. Most villages north of Fresnillo (near Zacatecas) had to be abandoned, and even haciendas survived only by becoming heavily fortified. Mexicans who were desperate to rid themselves of the Indian threat turned to adventurers such as Kirker to solve their problem.

called Father of the Independence; Ignacio Allende; Juan Aldama; and José Alfredo Jiménez. Later these heroes' bodies were exhumed and taken to Mexico City, where they were interred in the Monument a la Independencia. Another old cemetery, also now a park, is two blocks south and one block east from the first cemetery. Originally called the Pantéon de la Regla, it is now known as the Parque Revolución (H). This cemetery contains the mausoleum Pancho Villa bought to be buried in. He actually was buried in Parral, another city on the Camino Real, which you will visit later. Both cemeteries were in use during the 1840s and became the final resting place for many Americans who died here.

Back in the center of the city, you can visit the Museo de la Lealtad Republicana. Benito Juárez made this building his capitol during his residence in Chihuahua in the French occupation of Mexico, when Maximilian of Habsburg attempted to establish an empire with French support. The empire lasted from 1862 to 1867, but Juárez lived here only during the period 1864–66. The building, usually called simply La Casa de Juárez Museum, is located at Juárez and Calle 5 (C). It is worth a visit for its contents and the fact that the building itself is an early one.

You should also visit the dungeon, or cell, where Miguel Hidalgo y Costilla was held before being executed in 1811 (B). Padre Hidalgo had made his proclamation, his *grito*, on September 15, 1810, declaring independence for Mexico. This grito was made in the small town of Dolores, far to the south, which you will visit later on your tour. The padre and others in this insurrection were captured and brought to Chihuahua for later execution on July 30, 1811. The *"calabozo"* of don Miguel Hidalgo is under the post office, with its entrance on Avenida Juárez.

When in Chihuahua, it is difficult to avoid the ghost of Pancho Villa, a Durango native. Villa's career is postcamino, but he is revered in Chihuahua, and while you are here, you may want to learn more about his amazing life. The Museo de la Revolución (or Quinta Luz, for his wife, who inherited the house after his assassination) is at Calle 10 and Méndez (D), beyond Parque Lerdo. Exhibits include the car in which he was riding when he was shot in Parral, in southern Chihuahua state.

Another must-see attraction in Chihuahua is the colonial aqueduct, begun in 1751 to replace an earlier one built in 1706 (see Chihuahua city map for the aqueduct's location). This aqueduct brought water from the Río Chuviscar in the west to the city. To reach the aqueduct, drive southwest on Avenida Zarco to Calle Benitez. Once you find it, you can easily follow its course through the city.

The original mission settlements, Nombre de Dios and San Juan Bautista del Norte, can be visited by car (see Chihuahua city map for locations). From

An early photo by Ben Wittick of the aqueduct in Chihuahua.
Photo courtesy of the Palace of the Governors, Neg. No.: 15639.

downtown drive east on Calle Aldama to Avenida Colón and turn left, continuing over the Río Chuviscar. Continue under the bridge, and after the Santo Niño church, take a right on Escudero. Follow Escudero to Avenida Heroíco Colegio Militár. The Camino Real followed the latter avenida about one block to your right.

Continue north on Heroíco Militár, and on reaching a stoplight at Juan de Barrera, turn right. One block east is Calle 3a, which was the camino. Turn left here and go two blocks to Calle Fco. Marquez, turn left, and stop immediately at the church on your left. This is the site of the original settlement at Nombre de

Dios, founded in late 1690s. It was begun by the Franciscans to serve the local Indian population.

Turn around, return to Calle 3a, and go south about two blocks beyond where you entered at Barrera. The second mission settlement was at San Juan de Bautista, and it is to your southeast here. Go about two blocks south and then one east to find the church. This was another Franciscan mission settlement, the same age as Nombre de Dios. The present church is not the original.

Return to Colegio Militár and turn right, continuing north to Juan Escutia, where you should turn right again onto a road that will take you past the old Nombre de Dios plaza. Then you should turn left on the next block and continue north. In front of you, you will see the Quinta Carolina buildings, which are of interest but postcamino. This collection of buildings was the home of Luís Terrazas, governor of Chihuahua state from 1861–5, 1865–9, 1869–73, 1880–84, and 1903–4. The Quinta Carolina buildings, named for Terraza's wife, Carolina, are slowly being restored, but you can visit the church, which is still used for Sunday services and weddings.

Comments about the city of Chihuahua by traders are interesting and varied. Adolph Wislizenus, as he left the city for his forced exile to Cusihuiriáchic, called it "the sprightful city, which I had loved at first sight." Josiah Gregg says it was a magnificent place only if compared to Santa Fé and other places of the north. Gregg was, however, impressed with the town's aqueduct, which brought water to the public square.

+ + +

CHAPTER FIVE

Cusihuiriáchic to Zacatecas

+ + +

The Camino Real took several routes as it headed north from Durango toward Chihuahua. This guide suggests you travel southwest from Chihuahua on a route that will take you to Santa Bárbara and Parral. You can return north along the Río Conchos, which was the later route (described in chapter eight).

The area covered in this section is very important, since Oñate was forced to pause here for eighteen months while awaiting viceregal permission to move north into New Mexico. It was truly a frontier region in the late sixteenth century. The mines at Santa Bárbara and the fledgling agricultural area around Valle de San Bartolomé, where some of Oñate's hiatus was spent, were New Spain's most northerly sites. And these, remember, were situated many miles from the next settlements near Durango. This was dangerous, foreboding country.

You may also include a side trip to an almost-abandoned mining town to the west of Chihuahua. Adolph Wislizenus, with six other Americans, spent six months' exile in Cusihuiriáchic. An earlier visitor was Nicolás Lafora, on his inspection tour in 1767. The town is representative of the many failed mining ventures in northern New Spain.

Finally, there is the Basque-founded city of Durango. You will get a feeling of old Mexico here, and the beautiful plaza and striking physical setting are certain to interest all visitors. Durango is very cosmopolitan, with many seafood restaurants adding to this feeling. A fairly new highway runs from Durango to

Southern Chihuahua state

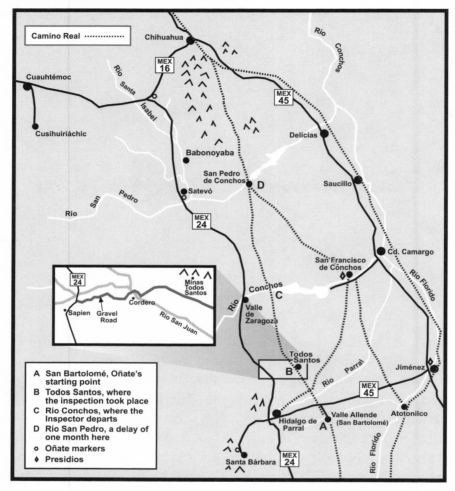

the Pacific coastal city of Mazatlán, which allows tropical and maritime products to enter the city.

Leave Chihuahua on México 16 and drive toward Cuauhtémoc. At KM 37, you approach the junction with México 24, which goes south to Parral. You will be returning to this junction later. On your left, just before the junction, is another Ruta de Oñate marker. Scholars are not certain of Oñate's exact route from Valle San Bartolomé to Chihuahua, because his journal was ambiguous about this area, but the valley of the Río Santa Isabel, which is a tributary of the Río San Pedro, is one possible route. After careful examination of the several

Mexican topographical maps covering this area and considerable fieldwork, the author is convinced that Oñate's route lay to the east of the mountains bordering the Río Santa Isabel.

CUSIHUIRIÁCHIC

Instead of turning south on México 24, you should continue to Ciudad Cuauhtémoc and visit the interesting silver-mining town of Cusihuiriáchic, or "Cusi," as it is called locally. Cusi was used as a place of internal exile for American traders at the time Colonel Doniphan's army was preparing to move south toward Chihuahua city. The best account of the town and this episode can be found in the journal of Adolph Wislizenus.

To get to Cusi, continue on México 16 to Ciudad Cuauhtémoc. It is about seventy kilometers (forty-two miles) from the junction with México 24 to Ciudad Cuauhtémoc on this toll road, with a booth at KM marker 68. The area around the city was settled by Mennonites who came to Canada from Europe, where they were being forced into military service, which their religion forbade. Then the Mexican government in the early 1920s welcomed them and allowed them to avoid military service. Still mainly rural, the Mennonites have formed communities with names such as Campo Veintiseis (Camp 26), which spread throughout this area. Their agricultural specialty, which is found everywhere, is cheese. Look for *queso mennonita* in markets, in stores, and along the highway.

When you reach Cuauhtémoc, look for the sign to the *centro*. This street, Avenida Lopez Rayón, will descend a hill and into the downtown area. Find the cross-street, Augustín Melgar, turn left there, and drive to Baja California, where you turn right. At Calle 30a, turn left and drive to Avenida Sonora, then turn right. This street will become Río Grijalva and lead you to Cusihuiriáchic. If you have trouble, just ask anyone for "Cusi" and they'll direct you there.

The road to Cusi goes by the large Mennonite Camp Veintiseis on your right. Just as the road begins a turn to the right, at El Mimbre, a road to the left will be going to Cusi. It's about five kilometers (three miles) from here to the edge of Cusi, which stretches for several miles along a narrow arroyo. Silver was discovered here in 1687, which led to a rush and the development of mines called El Milagro, San Carlos, San Rafael, and San Miguel. In a 1724 visit to Cusi, José Antonio de Villaseñor y Sánchez proclaimed that Real de Cusi was "one of the most opulent places of this province." The next mention of Cusi is found in Nicolás Lafora's account of April 4, 1767. Lafora wrote that one hundred families lived here with a priest and *alcalde mayor*. The population at that time consisted

Cusihuiriáchic

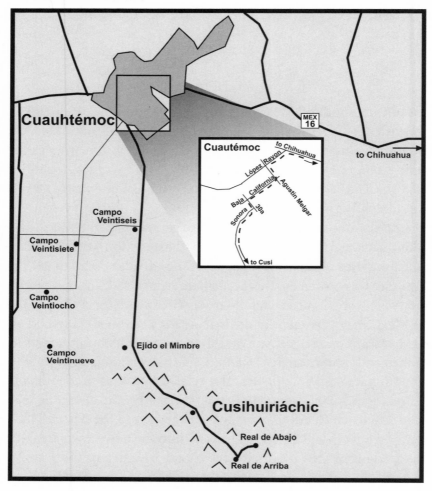

of "españoles, mestizos y mulatos" and some Indians who worked in the mines. He went on to say that the area was infested with Apaches who attacked at will.

In 1846 Adolph Wislizenus came south from Missouri by caravan with Albert Speyer, who had had two wagons with rifles destined for the governor at Chihuahua. General Kearny had sent troops out from Fort Leavenworth to find Speyer, but he was too fast for them. Speyer and Wislizenus (Wislizenus probably was unaware of the rifles) made it to Chihuahua with some adventures you can read about in the Wislizenus journal. Six Americans resident in the city of Chihuahua were arrested and sent to Cusihuiriáchic in September 1846, with

A few houses in Cusihuiriáchic are still occupied, but rows of abandoned buildings are more common in this once-thriving community. Photo by author.

Wislizenus following them a few days later. All were under a kind of "community arrest," with freedom to explore the immediate area. Wizlizenus's account of his six-month stay in Cusi is informative as well as amusing. He, too, spoke of Apache attacks but described the pursuit of the Apaches by the Americans and a few reluctant Mexicans in Cusi. The Mexicans, he says, are too fatalistic and won't put up a fight. His stay, like Susan Magoffin's in New Mexico, was filled with rumors about battles fought and not fought. He was able to return to Chihuahua on March 3, 1847, immediately after Doniphan's victory at Sacramento and the Mexican army's exodus from Chihuahua.

Cusihuiriáchic is built in a very narrow canyon with a small creek running through it. Today both sides of the only street are lined with mostly abandoned houses and stores. It is still the *cabecera*, or county seat, so a few municipal buildings are in the center of town. Toward the end of town, on the left, is a small museum. If it isn't open, and it usually isn't, return to the police station and ask one of the officers to open it for you. He will almost certainly comply with your request. (A small tip to the officer will help maintain the museum.) Continue down the

Juan de Oñate

Juan de Oñate's biographer called him the last conquistador, and that he certainly was. Oñate was born in about 1552, probably in the mining community of Zacatecas. His father, Cristóbal de Oñate, was one of the founders of Zacatecas in 1548, barely two years after the discovery of its rich silver ore. Cristóbal Oñate owned several silver mines at Pánuco, a town about five miles north of Zacatecas, at the very northern end of the mining district, which was considered a suburb of Zacatecas. For the many details concerning the life of Juan de Oñate, you should consult Marc Simmons's *The Last Conquistador*. You will also be directed to the Oñate hacienda in Pánuco later.

In 1550 Zacatecas was not a contiguous extension of the Spanish-occupied territory. It lay two hundred miles north of Guadalajara, whence its founders had come. It was, in fact, an island of occupation for many years, surrounded by hostile indigenous people, the Chichimecas. Even when Zacatecas itself had enough miners and tradespeople to afford a defense, the 250-mile trip from Zacatecas to Querétaro was a hazardous one. Since the route established after 1550, the Camino de la Plata (the Silver Road), passed through the homelands of several hostile Indian tribes, young Oñate spent his childhood constantly reminded of danger and heroism. With another home in Mexico City, young Juan certainly made many trips on the Camino de la Plata.

Spaniards living in sixteenth-century America had a unique worldview, one conditioned by recent Spanish history. Stories of the conquest of southern Iberia and the expulsion of the Moors in 1492, coupled with the amazing conquest of Mexico in 1521, certainly instilled a great sense of pride and accomplishment in young Spaniards such as Oñate and inspired a confidence in their ability to succeed in almost anything.

Achieving adulthood and with the inherited mines prospering, Oñate was eager for a challenge. He proposed leading a group of settlers and clergy to New Mexico, a province well known by the late 1500s as a result of the expedition of Vásquez de Coronado in the early 1540s and of some others in the 1580s and 1590s. Their accounts of substantial numbers of Indians living in New Mexico who had

canyon until you reach a fork. The left fork leaves the canyon floor; the right crosses the creek and takes you to a church. After visiting the church, you should turn around and head back to Cuauhtémoc and the highway.

When you arrive at the highway in Cuauhtémoc, turn right on México 16 to return to the aforementioned junction with México 24. At the junction turn multistoried houses and were sedentary farmers enticed churchmen and settlers to conquer New Mexico and convert the heathen Indians to Christianity. Another motive was certainly the dream of becoming wealthy by finding a mother lode of gold or silver. Why should the last great strike be at Zacatecas and not in New Mexico?

Oñate's expedition was authorized in 1595, but he was delayed until 1598 while a last-minute supplicant sought to replace him. This challenge was overcome in 1597, when he finally started north with his large caravan from Durango, traveling to the banks of the Río Nazas, the mines of Caxco, and finally the Valle de San Bartolomé (in present southernmost Chihuahua state) in November 1597.

At San Bartolomé, the viceregal inspector, Juan de Frías Salazar, directed Oñate to move his caravan north for the final inspection. Salazar was certain that Oñate would use residents of San Bartolomé in an attempt to increase his count of settlers. As it turned out, Oñate did come up short and had to post a bond guaranteeing to provide more settlers later. The inspection was held near the Todos Santos mines, about two days' travel north of San Bartolomé, and took one month. Then on January 26, 1598, Oñate's three-mile-long caravan moved north once again.

When the caravan reached the Río Conchos, the water was running high, but Oñate challenged his men to cross. It was here that the hated inspector took his leave without ceremony, to the great consternation of Oñate and his men. Their next stop was at the Río San Pedro, thirty miles north. At this point, Oñate paused for one month, waiting for a group of tardy friars. He also sent Vicente de Zaldívar ahead with a small contingent of troops to seek out the best route, one his carts could use that provided water for the livestock. Luckily for Oñate, Zaldívar succeeded in finding a good, well-watered route.

What adjectives best describe the conquistador? *Determined, brave,* and *courageous* all fit Oñate. But what about a leader who took all of those men, women, children, carts, and livestock through an area that was truly unknown? One could add to the list of adjectives *foolhardy, reckless,* and *audacious.* Whatever we think of him, his effort extended the Camino Real 750 miles from San Bartolomé to San Juan Pueblo in New Mexico.

right and head toward Parral. The road you are on parallels the Río Santa Isabel and meets the Río Satevó farther along. At first you are to the east of the river, and then crossing it puts you on a ridge between the Ríos Santa Isabel and Satevó. You will see in the river valley to your left the small town of Babonoyaba, one of the few old towns along this route. Mexican scholars, unlike the author, place this town on the route that Oñate would have followed if he came up the Santa Isabel valley. To visit Babonoyaba, turn left at about KM 36 and drive about ten kilometers (six miles), keeping to the right at the only road junction. This attractive village has a very nice 1665 church.

At about KM marker 48, having descended the ridge, you will approach the Río Satevó, a tributary of the Río San Pedro. At a Ruta de Oñate marker next to the Pemex station on the left, turn left to visit the attractive town of Satevó near-by. In front of the church, which was built by the Jesuits and dates from 1640, some historical markers will tell you about the church and the Satevó area. Lafora passed through Satevó in 1767 and wrote that it was inhabited by "some gente de razón [non-Indians] and Tepehuanes Indians." He made no mention of the church but said that Satevó was under the curate at Babonoyaba, four leagues (sixteen miles) away.

A few kilometers beyond Satevó, you will cross the Río San Pedro. Oñate crossed this stream, perhaps forty kilometers (twenty-four miles) east of this point. He had to wait at the San Pedro crossing for one month until a group of tardy friars caught up. Vicente Zaldívar was sent north to seek a good route for his caravan. From this point on, Oñate was blazing a new trail, since earlier parties heading for New Mexico had relied on the Río Conchos for their trips. Zaldívar was to find a route for the carts and, more importantly, locate water sources.

Return to the highway and continue south toward Parral. At KM marker 120, you pass over the Río Conchos, the state's second-most important river after the Rio Grande (called the Río Bravo in Mexico). A few kilometers before reaching the Río Conchos, Lafora mentions crossing the Camino Real de Chihuahua. This route, which the author has not located thus far, was likely a western route used from Parral to Chihuahua. Lafora mentioned a hacienda, Nuestra Señora del Pilar, at this point when he passed through in April 1767. He said that it was thir-ty leagues, about 120 miles, from the presidio on the Río Conchos. The presidio he referred to was the one at San Francisco de Conchos, which you will visit later on your trip north. Oñate crossed the Río Conchos about halfway between here and the site of the future presidio. When his caravan reached the Conchos on February 7, 1598, the river was running high. According to his chronicler, Captain Gaspar Pérez de Villagrá, Oñate encouraged his entourage by bravely fording the river on his horse. This was also the point at which Oñate was rid of his hated inspector, Juan de Frías Salazar, for at this point Salazar returned south.

Continue south on México 24, watching for KM 149. Just beyond this mark-er lies a small arroyo and, beyond that, on the left, a gravel road that you should take. You will pass by a ranch on your left, and at about eight kilometers (five miles) from the highway, you will see a ranch complex among some trees on your right. This is Cordero, about where the inspection of Juan de Oñate's caravan took place. Oñate and caravan arrived here on December 20, 1597, and the inspection concluded on January 26, 1598, on which date he left for New Mexico with the hated inspector Salazar in tow. Oñate took one day to arrive at the Todos Santos mines. To see the mines, continue past Cordero, keeping to the right, and you will see some hills to your front left. If you look carefully, you can see mine scars on the side of the hills. It is not worth going beyond here because the gate at the mine road is locked. Return to México 24 and continue toward Parral.

PARRAL

You eventually will see Parral, officially named Hidalgo del Parral, to your left front. With many good places to stay, Parral is a good location for a headquarters for several short day trips (see appendix). Once the silver mines were opened in 1631 on the site of an earlier hacienda, Nuestra Señora del Parral, Parral immediately became an important city and was, in fact, the de facto capital of Nueva Vizcaya for some time. From here it is possible to visit the mining town of Santa Bárbara and the Oñate jumping-off point Valle de San Bartolomé, now called Valle de Allende. Pedro Rivera, who visited Parral on an inspection tour in 1726, commented that it had "considerable mining in times past" and noted that at that time, it was the residence of the governor and *capitán general* of Nueva Vizcaya.

To get to Santa Bárbara, leave on México 32 from the southwest part of Parral. A few miles beyond the city, you will see the highway to Santa Bárbara. As you approach the center of town, you will see more Ruta de Oñate markers on your right, including one with a nice map. Silver was first discovered here in 1567, but due to a shortage of labor, the mines couldn't be worked intensively at that time. The population of central Mexico had declined from about 15 million in 1521 to 1.5 million in 1625, with the result that there were few surplus Indians to send north to labor in the mines. Mining was not just a matter of digging into the ground. Mines called for labor, food, and fuel. Food was produced nearby at places such as Valle de San Bartolomé. Local ranches provided meat as well as many other products from cattle. Hides were used to make buckets and ropes, while the tallow was used for candles. Additionally, mules and burros were needed to carry ore and pull carts and mix the ore in the mining patios. At the time of discovery of silver in the late 1500s, Santa Bárbara was probably too far from the main body of New Spain to thrive.

PARRAL TO ZACATECAS

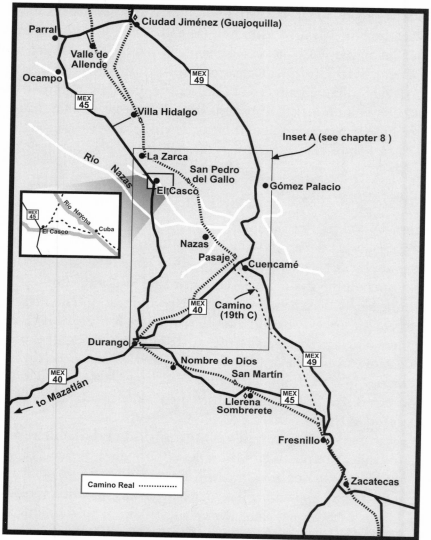

Go all the way through town, crossing the stream, and find your way to the pretty church on the left. This church, called Santa Bárbara Parish, was begun in 1571, when the town had but thirty miners and merchants. From here return to the Parral highway. If you wish, you can visit the mining town of San Francisco del Oro. To get there, turn left on México 32 and follow the signs. San Francisco is a little younger than is Santa Bárbara, its date of founding set at 1658. Both towns still have a small amount of mining activity.

Mining of Silver

A short description of mining processes is necessary to understand the organization of mining ventures in the region of the Camino Real as well as the impact of the mining on other areas. Almost every writer passing through northern Mexico spoke of the *patio* method of silver extraction. This system was one of amalgamation, joining silver with mercury. Ore was first crushed, then mixed with mercury, salt, copper sulfate, and water to make a slurry. Over several months, the silver compounds of the ore were converted to metallic silver, which formed an amalgam with the mercury. When the chemical process was complete, the heavier alloy of silver and mercury would sink to the bottom, allowing it to be separated from the lighter waste. The amalgam of silver and mercury was then heated to drive off the mercury and recapture it. This was simply a distillation process. What was left was almost pure silver.

Two outside agents, mercury and salt, were government monopolies, with the sole source of mercury being mines in Spain. This control of essential elements in the amalgamation process meant that Spain was certain to get its fair share, the royal fifth, or *quinta real*, of the silver.

Another method of extraction was less common but no less important. Rich silver ore could be smelted. This system was far less capital intensive, so many merchants and workers had small smelters on their property to refine either legal or stolen ores. Smelting was most efficient when lead was included in the ore, either as galena or introduced from lead mines as what is called litharge. Local forests suffered under either system but far more with smelting, which called for substantial amounts of charcoal.

When the ores of Zacatecas were discovered in 1546, smelting was the only process the Spanish had. The amalgamation process, the patio method, was introduced into New Spain by Bartolomé de Medina, who had learned about it from a German in Spain and came to Mexico to make his fortune showing miners the new process. The new system was first used in 1554 at the mines at Pachuca, a town one hundred kilometers (sixty miles) north of Mexico City. In smelting, miners knew, silver ore had to assay at least ten ounces per hundred pounds of ore to be economically feasible. With the amalgamation process, however, the breaking point was one-tenth of that. The rush to Zacatecas would have been short-lived without the miracle of amalgamation.

SAN BARTOLOMÉ

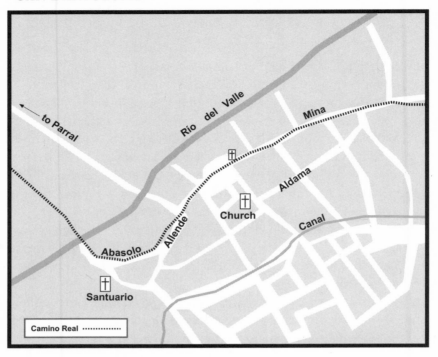

VALLE DE SAN BARTOLOMÉ
(NOW VALLE DE ALLENDE)

From Parral the trip to Valle de Allende requires that you head east toward Jiménez on México 45. This road is a newly completed toll road, but the toll booth is beyond our turnoff. At KM marker 23, turn right (south) toward Valle de Allende, on Highway 73. From the highway, you will descend into the valley, where you will first cross a small river and then enter the town. Originally called Valle de San Bartolomé, this was the northernmost agricultural settlement in New Spain in the late sixteenth century. By 1570 the community already had a convent; thus, it had taken the Spaniards less than sixty years to expand from the Valley of Mexico to this point. A truly amazing feat.

The camino, whose route is shown on the accompanying map, entered town from the east on Mina, passed by the plaza and church, and crossed the small stream by way of Abásolo. Others suggest that the camino entered from the south on Avenida Cuahtémoc and descended the hill, passing the church and plaza.

The scene is of the Camino Real departing San Bartolomé. Juan de Oñate certainly used this very route in 1598. Photo by author.

Juan de Oñate and his caravan stayed in San Bartolomé from August 19, 1597, to December of the same year. It was here that Juan de Frías Salazar, the inspector, arriving in early November, finally caught up with the caravan and ordered Oñate to move the caravan north immediately. Regardless of Salazar's impatience, however, the caravan could not move without considerable preparation and did not leave San Bartolomé until December 17, 1597. Three days later, the inspection began at the site (Cordero) you visited earlier.

The San Bartolomé community was founded by the Franciscans in the 1560s, at about the time the Santa Bárbara mines were established. In its early days, San Bartolomé functioned as an administrative and supply center, and at one time, it had a presidio. Farms growing wheat and corn were situated up and down the valley. The town today is a wonder. Pecan trees shade the streets and the plaza adjacent to the river. The town appears almost unchanged since Juan de Oñate's visit in 1597. Be sure to visit the crossing point of the river as you follow Abásolo west.

After seeing Valle de Allende, you should return to the highway and turn back toward Parral. Just a few kilometers after you rejoin México 45, at about

Abandoned hacienda San Gregorio, just north of San Bartolomé on the Parral River. Photo by author.

KM 15, take the road to your right to "Estación Adele" if you wish to visit the crossing point of the Río Parral. In just a few miles, you will begin the descent to the river, and the first thing you will see is the ruined church of the hacienda to your right. This is the Hacienda San Gregorio, directly on the Camino Real. Return to the highway, turn right toward Parral, and look for signs directing you toward Durango on México 45.

From here to Durango is 436 kilometers (262 miles), a day's drive with a few stops. On the map, you will see several sites on the Camino Real to the east of México 45, the road you will take to Durango. This guide is arranged so that you will visit those sites on your return north from Zacatecas. Information on those sites is found in chapter eight.

Sixty-three kilometers (37.8 miles) south of Parral on México 45, you will arrive at the small town of Villa Ocampo. Originally named San Miguel de las Bocas, Ocampo was settled in 1630, on the Río Florido. Food was raised here for the mines at Santa Bárbara, San Francisco de Oro, and Parral. You'll visit the Río Florido again at Jiménez on your trip north. The small stream you forded in San Bartolomé is a tributary of the Florido.

CERRO GORDO
(NOW VILLA HIDALGO)

At about eighty kilometers (forty-eight miles) south of Ocampo, you will come to a junction for Villa Hidalgo (originally Cerro Gordo). You can't miss it because the Mexican army usually has a checkpoint at this intersection. Turn left toward Villa Hidalgo. As you drive east, you will see Cerro Gordo (Fat Peak), the large peak for which the town was originally named, straight ahead. It will be approximately twenty kilometers (twelve miles) before you come to a reservoir, pass over the dam, and enter the small town.

This community was named San Miguel de Cerro Gordo in 1648 when it was established as a presidio. The location was chosen in response to the Tarahumara revolts between 1645 and 1652. And it wasn't only the Tarahumaras but also the Tabosos to the east and Conchos from the north that were threatening settlements in this area.

Pedro Rivera arrived at Cerro Gordo on the eleventh day of November 1725. He wrote that the presidio was sited on a deep arroyo with sufficient water to supply the garrison and a hacienda on the opposite bank. By the time of Nicolás Lafora's inspection visit in May 1766, the presidio was "extinguished." The next year, however, the presidio had been reformed, and the Marqués de Rubí wrote in his journal that on the trip south, he visited "the new presidio of Cerro Gordo, which was established after my first trip through the pueblo of the same name." Soon afterward, this presidio was moved to the spring of San Carlos on the Rio Grande, a shift resulting from the very inspection that Rubí and Lafora were engaged in. The new presidio on the Rio Grande was to become part of the Line.

Josiah Gregg passed through Cerro Gordo in 1835 without comment. James Josiah Webb, in 1846, wrote that since it was a frontier town between the states of Durango and Chihuahua, the trains had to show their *guias* (passports) here. He had little trouble at Cerro Gordo going south, but the customs officials gave him grief on his return north.

As you enter town today, from the south, the road tees at a small square in front of the municipal building. Turn right here to view the church, San Miguel Arcángel, and the old plaza one block away. The date on the front of the church is hard to read, but it seems to be in the late 1700s. The presidio walls, which would have included this church and plaza, aren't visible today. Continue to your left around the plaza, returning to the municipal building on the side opposite your entry into town. Park in the area. Looking back across the small

Traces of the camino can still be seen in the pavement here in Villa Hidalgo. Originally known as Cerro Gordo, it was a once-thriving town with a presidio. Villa Hidalgo is now a somnolent village. Photo by author.

square to ascertain the road you entered on, locate a road to the north that would form a continuation of that road. This road drops into the arroyo to the north. If you inspect the roadbed carefully, you will see that the stones were placed to form pavement. This is the Camino Real or, as a man living on it called it, el Camino de los Carros. Today it is Calle las Diligencias.

Leaving Villa Hidalgo, return to México 45 and turn left toward Durango. Fifty kilometers (thirty miles) from this intersection, a road on your left leads to La Zarca. La Zarca, according to Gregg, was a hacienda of large proportions. He said it was one hundred miles in length. Rivera in 1725 and Lafora in 1766 both mention La Zarca. Josiah Webb tells the story of the twenty-one Americans in his party who bought mules in La Zarca (it was noted for fine horses and mules) before leaving his caravan in the hope of joining General Wool in Monclova. Doniphan and his forces moved south from El Paso del Norte, thinking they would link up with General Wool. Just south of La Zarca, the twenty-one, under their elected leader, David McCoy of Westport, Missouri, headed east over the Bolsón de Mapimí. This *bolsón*, or large pocket, is still virtually unpopulated (it's

Casco was where Juan de Oñate spent nine months in 1597, waiting for word from the king to move north. Photo by author.

called the Silent Zone) and devoid of water and pasturage. Half the party perished, and the rest made it to the town of Guajoquilla. You will read that part of the story on your return trip north in chapter eight.

To get to the village, go east a few kilometers and turn north, following signs. Today it is a nondescript village, and the hacienda (the proper name for the walled collection of buildings is *casco*; the landed estate is called a hacienda) is nowhere in view. Return to México 45 and turn left again toward Durango. In about 31 kilometers (18.6 miles), you approach El Casco on the river of the same name. The pueblo of El Casco is just past KM marker 209 and to your left.

The first mention of Casco is found in Oñate's record of his march north from Zacatecas in 1596. There he writes of the "mines of Casco, in the government of New Viscaya." Oñate had received the very bad news of his possibly being replaced as *adelantado* by another Spaniard while he was at the crossing of the Río Nazas, south of Casco. He later convinced the authorities to allow his caravan to move north to Casco, where there were adequate pastures for his livestock.

Thus we find Oñate and caravan in the Casco area from November 1, 1596, to August 1, 1597. The news that Oñate was, in fact, to receive the king's blessing came to him here at Casco in the summer of 1597. Oñate left Casco on August 1, 1597, after a stay of nine months.

Some abandoned mines are just east of the present village of Casco, but the pasturage that Oñate's stock (perhaps as many as seven hundred head of livestock) needed was spread down this valley at least as far as the Río Casco's confluence with the Río Naycha. You can follow a decent gravel road from Casco that meets the pavement between San Luís Cordero and Gallo, but this guide directs you south on México 45 to Durango, covering those eastern sites on your way north in chapter eight.

Return to México 45 and continue to Durango.

Durango

As you approach Durango, look for signs directing you to Centro, the center of the city. The cathedral and Plaza de Armas are both situated on 20 de Noviembre. (The hotel listing in the appendix notes a hotel in the downtown area.)

Durango, first named Guadiana, was sited in 1563 by another intrepid Basque, Francisco de Ibarra. This Ibarra was a nephew of one of the four founders of Zacatecas, Diego de Ibarra. It was, in fact, the uncle's silver-mining money that financed Francisco's exploration of the Guadiana valley.

Pedro Rivera, on his tour of 1725, did not have a great deal to say about Durango except that it was the capital of Nueva Vizcaya and had a *real de hacienda* (mint). He described the makeup of the citizens as *"españoles, mestizos y mulatos."* Nicolás Lafora, on his visit in 1766, had an expanded description of the city. He counted three convents (Franciscan, Augustinian, and Jesuit) in addition to parish churches and the cathedral. Lafora stated that there were thirteen hundred families of españoles, mulatos, and mestizos and a quarter, or section, with ninety-five families of Indians.

Josiah Gregg visited Durango in 1835 but said he made a detour off the usual road (Camino Real) to get to the city. The camino by that time struck north from Fresnillo to Cuencamé, and it was at the latter city that Gregg left the camino. Calling Durango one of the handsomest cities in the north, with two or three attractive plazas and some twenty thousand residents, Gregg noted the many scorpions in the area, which young boys collected to get a reward of three cents per scorpion.

Another visitor was James Josiah Webb in 1846. He did not describe the city but did write that Comanches were marauding near the city, stealing cattle,

DURANGO

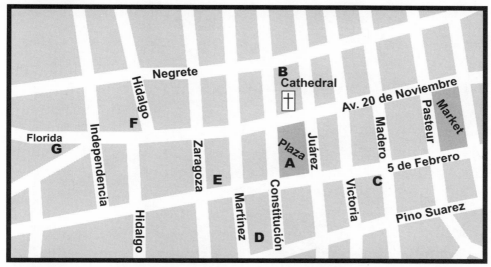

KEY

A Plaza de Armas
B Cathedral
C Casa del Conde del Valle de Durango
D University of Juárez of Durango

E Palace of Government
F Templo de San Agustín
G State Tourism Office

horses, and mules with impunity. He remained in Durango ten days and makes a good witness to events. George Ruxton, a British citizen traveling north on the camino in 1846, describes Comanche attacks that occurred between Durango and Zacatecas.

Today Durango is a very pleasant city for a visit. Start with the Plaza de Armas (A on map) on 20 de Noviembre, across from the cathedral. From the plaza, cross 20 de Noviembre to the cathedral (B). The church you see today was started in 1635 but not finished until two hundred years had passed. From the cathedral, walk east to Francisco Madero and south to 5 de Febrero. Here you will see the Casa del Conde del Valle de Súchil (C), a colonial house constructed in 1763 and 1764 and owned by a wealthy miner, Joseph del Campo Soberón y Larrea. Nearby, on the site of the Colegio de la Compañía de Jesús, is the University of Juárez of Durango (D) (on Bruno Martínez). The *colegio* dates from the sixteenth century, and part of the original colegio is incorporated in the university.

The Palace of Government (E), on 5 de Febrero, occupies a beautiful building that was originally the home of the miner José Zambrano. The original town plan shows the government palace on the block immediately south of the Plaza

The cathedral in Durango. Durango is the capital of the state of the same name but was once the capital of all of Nueva Vizcaya. Photo by author.

de Armas, where we would expect it to be. Finally, the Templo de San Agustín, founded by the first bishop of Durango in 1637, is at the corner of Avenida 20 de Noviembre and Calle Hidalgo (F).

There is more to see in Durango, but the buildings mentioned above are representative of the time of the colonial Camino Real and a time when the bishop of Durango had all of the north in his charge. If you wish to see more of the city, visit the state tourism office on Florida (G) to get maps and more information.

It was from Durango that Bishop Tamarón left to make his inspection trip to New Mexico in 1760. Also, Jean Lamy, having been appointed bishop of New Mexico, made the trek to Durango to seek that bishop's approval of sorts.

Willa Cather's novel *Death Comes for the Archbishop* tells the fictionalized story in great detail.

Leave Durango on México 45 heading toward Zacatecas. In 57 kilometers (34.2 miles), you will arrive at Nombre de Dios, another town founded by Francisco de Ibarra in 1563. It never was a very large town: Lafora in 1766 said its population was reduced to a few mulatos and eight hundred *"indios mexicanos,"* who must have been Indians brought north from around Mexico City to be farmers or mine workers. Today turn right from the highway when you see the church spire on the *plaza principal* (main plaza). This church, the Templo de Jesús Nazareno, dates from the seventeenth century. The church in ruins nearby is the Templo de San Francisco, which was built in 1564, almost simultaneous with the town's founding.

SOMBRERETE

Return to México 45, turn right, and continue toward Zacatecas until you reach the turn for Sombrerete, just after crossing into the state of Zacatecas. Sombrerete, founded by don Juan de Tolosa, another of the four Basque founders of Zacatecas, was named after a nearby hill that looked similar to the tricorner hat (*sombrero* is "hat" in Spanish) popular in the sixteenth century. The official name was La Villa de Llerena or Real de Minas de Sombrerete.

SOMBRERETE

KEY
A Capilla de la Tercera Orden
B Templo de San Francisco
C Ex-Convento de San Mateo

Rivera, visiting Sombrerete in 1725, noted that in times past, it was thriving, but at the time of his visit, only a third of the houses were occupied as a result of mines closing. Lafora noted much the same in 1766, when only one mine, La Norte, was still open.

Go to the center of town and park. Ask for the Plaza de San Francisco, which is a two-block walk from the tourist office. On the plaza, you will see to the left the Templo de San Francisco, built at the conclusion of the seventeenth century, and the *Ex-convento* de San Mateo, founded in about 1560.

Return to México 45 and continue southeast toward Fresnillo. Sombrerete and Fresnillo both had presidios at the time the Chichimeca Wars were fought throughout the Zacatecas area, from 1550 until about 1600. The Spaniards used presidios to protect towns, mines, and the Camino Real. Needless to say, this strategy did not work better here than it did anywhere else.

Continue to Zacatecas.

✝   ✝   ✝

CHAPTER SIX

Zacatecas and the Silver Road

✝   ✝   ✝

ZACATECAS

The story of northern Mexico must begin with the city of Zacatecas. One historian wrote that the foundation of the city was a "pregnant historical moment." Discovery of silver ore at Zacatecas occurred quite by accident in September 1546, when Captain Juan de Tolosa and some soldiers camped below Cerro de la Bufa, the large hill east of the present city. Local Indians, Zacatecos, showed him some ore that proved to be about half silver. The rest, as they say, is history.

Later, on January 20, 1548, four men, Juan de Tolosa, Cristóbal de Oñate, Diego de Ibarra, and Báltasar Temiño de Bañuelos, met under La Bufa to formalize the founding of Zacatecas. The name *Zacatecas* is from *zacatl*, "grass," and *tecatl*, "people," the Aztec descriptive name for the local Indians.

Even with firm knowledge that the hills around Zacatecas were truly saturated with silver, the community had rough going for its first few years. Only when a sufficient number of men gathered at the mines was it safe from Indian attack. It began to prosper, but even then, 1549–50, the town was an oasis separated by many miles from the next Spanish settlements. Improvements had to be made in transportation so that the miners could be fed and supplied with necessary equipment and, importantly, so that refined silver could be transported to Mexico City. Thus was the Camino de la Plata constructed south to Querétaro and on to the capital.

Zacatecas in the 1600s

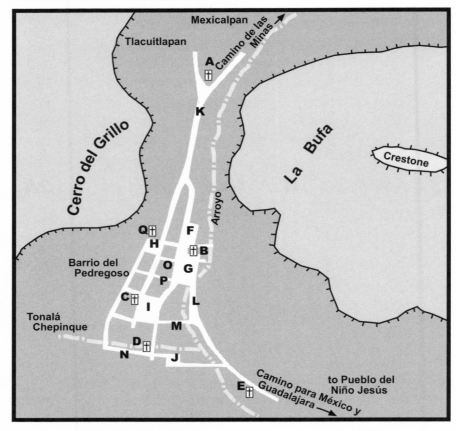

After P. J. Bakewell, Silver Mining and Society in Colonial Mexico, Zacatecas, 1546–1700

KEY

A Convento de San Francisco
B Iglesia mayor *(the parish church)*
C Convento de San Agustín
D Convento y Hospital de
  San Juan de Dios
E Convento de Santo Domingo
F Plazuela dal Maestre de Campo
G Plaza publica
H Plaza de Santa Domigo
  (modern name)
I Plazuela de San Agutín

J Plaza de Villareal
  (end of 17th century)
K Calle de San Francisco
L Calle de Tacuba
M Calle de los Zapateros
N Calle de los Gorreros
O Casa Reales
  (casa de cabildo, carcel)
P Real Caja
Q Colegio de la Sociedad de Jesús

Aqueduct in Zacatecas. Photo by author.

Zacatecas began as a typical mining town. Mines were everywhere around the arroyo in which the town sits. La Bufa was closest, but the richest strike was at Veta Grande (large vein) north of the town, followed by the mines at Pánuco, even farther north from Veta Grande. Silver at Pánuco was discovered in November 1548, which became home to the Oñate family, first Cristóbal, then his son Juan.

Mines need labor, food, and equipment, so Zacatecas became a supply center for the local mines as well as for the mines opened later at Fresnillo, Sombrerete, and San Martín. Development of a "plan" for the city was impossible. The site was in a narrow arroyo hemmed in by cerros, hills, on three sides. The city in the 1660s had a parroquia church (where the cathedral is today), several roads with the road to the north marked Camino de las Minas going to Pánuco, and the old hacienda of the Oñate family. There was also a panoply of convents built by the various religious orders. Calle de Tacuba, found on both Zacatecas maps, was the route that led to Tacuba near Mexico City and on to the mint in the city by way of Calle Tacuba.

La Bufa behind the cathedral in Zacatecas. Photo by author.

Two visitors, Pedro de Rivera in 1724 and Nicolás Lafora in 1766, had surprisingly little to say about Zacatecas. Rivera did note the arroyo running through town and said a major flood inundated it in 1722. Lafora wrote that the mines were in decline at the time of his visit, which had led to declining population. He listed the parroquia and five convents, as well as a Jesuit colegio, which was very rich, according to him.

The best location to begin a visit to the sites in Zacatecas is at the cathedral. It was built beginning in 1729, on the site of the earlier parroquia church (this and most other places can be located on the accompanying map from the 1600s). The adjacent Plaza de Armas is of modest dimensions for such an important place (remember how grand the Plaza de Armas is in Durango). There simply was no space for a large plaza in this narrow canyon. To the east, behind the Plaza de Armas, is the Palacio de Gobierno, built in the eighteenth

ZACATECAS

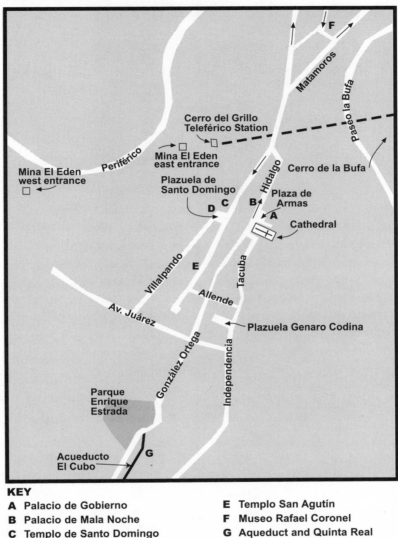

KEY

A Palacio de Gobierno
B Palacio de Mala Noche
C Templo de Santo Domingo
D Museo Pedro Coronel

E Templo San Agutín
F Museo Rafael Coronel
G Aqueduct and Quinta Real

century. West of the plaza, across the street, is the Palacio de Mala Noche, an eighteenth-century home.

Climbing the hill to the west of Calle Hidalgo uphill one street and turning left will bring you to the Plazuela de Santo Domingo. The church of Santo Domingo was actually built in the 1740s by the Jesuits, who assigned it to the

El Bracho was the earliest church in Zacatecas, dating from 1550. Photo by author.

Dominicans in 1767 when they were expelled from the New World. The church is on this small plaza. Adjacent to the church is the Museo Pedro Coronel, housed in the seventeenth-century Jesuit college.

Continue south on Dr. Hierro several blocks to the Templo de Agustín. The Augustinian friars arrived in Zacatecas in 1575. This church was built in the seventeenth century but was converted into a casino during the anticlerical fervor in the nineteenth century. It had yet another life when, in 1882, it was purchased by American Presbyterian missionaries, who made extensive changes to the building. It has since been returned to the Catholic church.

One of Mexico's most attractive aqueducts can be reached by a short walk from downtown. Go south on Hidalgo (the street in front of the cathedral), passing Avenida Juárez and climbing a gentle hill and then descending past

Parque Enrique Estrada on your right. Here, where the aqueduct ends, you'll see it coming in from the south. Called Acueducto del Cubo, it was built in the eighteenth century to bring water from the mine El Cubo to the southern portion of the city. Also nearby is the old bull ring, now the hotel Quinta Real, expensive but with a reasonably priced restaurant and very good food. It is worth visiting the hotel just to see the interior of the bull ring.

You will find two other activities in the downtown area. First, you can tour the *mina* El Eden, which was a very important silver mine during colonial and later times. One of its seven levels is kept open for visitors. There are two mine entrances, as shown on the accompanying map. Another activity is to use the *teleférico* (cable car) to ascend to La Bufa. The entrance to the teleférico is very near the east entrance of the El Eden mine.

It is now time to get in your car and visit sites outside the city. Take Hidalgo north past the Plaza de Armas and continue past a fountain, where the name of the street changes to Matamoros. A few hundred yards past the fountain, on your left, will be the Museo Rafael Coronel. This museum is in the old convento de San Francisco, built first in 1569 but destroyed by fire in 1648. Reconstruction began immediately after the fire.

Continue winding your way up the valley, and you eventually will pass under the *periférico*, the highway that circles the city. You will use the periférico later in this auto tour. After crossing under it, you'll see dozens of buses parked, waiting to return to the center of town. At this point, take the left road or, more accurately, the one straight ahead, which will take you to El Bracho. As you follow this road north, you will see on your right front a small church, Capilla El Bracho, built in 1549 and the oldest building in Zacatecas. The immediate area is likely where the first settlements were since many of the mines were nearby.

PÁNUCO

From El Bracho, return to where the buses were parked and turn left, heading up the hill. At the top, turn left and follow signs to Veta Grande. Veta Grande is today a small town with what appears to be a working mine. Just as you arrive at the edge of Veta Grande, you will see a Pemex station and a sign directing you to the right to Pánuco. Ignore the sign and go straight ahead. Pánuco is about five kilometers (three miles) farther along.

When you enter Pánuco, head for the church and plaza. You will see the library and municipal building on one side of the plaza. Take the street on which the municipal building is situated to the right (northeast). The road degenerates

ZACATECAS TO PÁNUCO

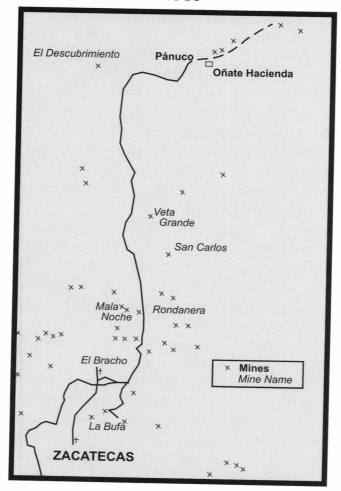

somewhat but is still passable by passenger vehicle. In a few hundred yards, you'll see the stone walls of a *casco* (the proper name for the walled-in collection of buildings) on your left. Continue past the walls to an opening, turn left into the casco, and park.

This is the casco of the Oñate family. Cristóbal Oñate, one of the founders of Zacatecas, owned mines in the Pánuco area. The local librarian told the author that one mine, Descubrimiento, which is just west of town, was the major mine of the Oñates'. Juan de Oñate was born in about 1550, perhaps in Zacatecas, and likely inherited this hacienda from Cristóbal when the father died in 1567.

Plan of the Oñate casco

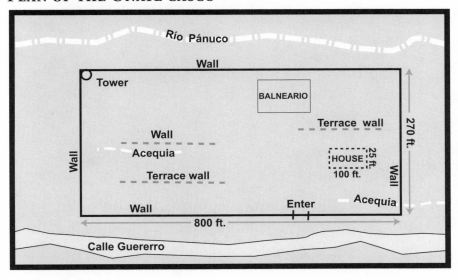

The largest tower remaining at the Oñate casco. Photo by author.

The casco is an impressive site. The ruins of the home are seen near the entry passage on the south. It was not a very large house, but it was likely the family residence for only part of the year, since the Oñates had a home in Mexico City as well. In the southeast corner of the casco, you can detect the acequia, which leads from a now silted-up *presa*, or dam, upstream. It is an easy walk to the dam along the route of the acequia.

Panorama of the Oñate casco in Pánuco. The walled towers are evident, and the small stream can be seen at the lower-right side of photo. Photo by author.

After visiting the casco, return toward the city the way you came, but turn left just before the periférico to climb the hill to La Bufa. The best part of La Bufa is the view, since you can look almost directly down on the city center. You can also see El Bracho and the small community surrounding it. And, for the last time perhaps, you will come into contact with the intrepid Pancho Villa. Villa and his División del Norte (Northern Division) captured the city after a battle on La Bufa with federal troops on June 23, 1914. You can see a statue of Villa and visit a museum with extensive displays of the battle. Few Mexican cities are without an Avenida "División del Norte."

Return to the downtown by descending La Bufa on the same road you used to get to the top. Get onto the periférico going west. Look for a sign to Colonia Díaz Ordaz and turn left to go down the hill. Just a few blocks after leaving the periférico, the road veers left (on Boulevard María Esther), and you should stop here and park your car. Walk the short block down the hill (this is another one-way "up" street) to a church on your right. This is likely the city's second-oldest church, Capilla de Mexicalpan, situated in one of the sixteenth-century Indian barrios. Recall that the Spaniards had to import Indians from the south to farm and work in the mines.

Go back to your car and complete the descent into Zacatecas. It is a difficult city to get around in but makes good practice for Guanajuato, which you will visit later and is even more difficult.

The Camino Real followed two routes south of Zacatecas. You will be directed south toward Mexico City closely following the original 1550 Camino de la Plata. This route goes southeast from Zacatecas through Ojuelos, Dolores Hidalgo, San Miguel, and Querétaro. On your return north from Mexico City, you will follow the later Camino Real, through Celaya and Aguascalientes to Zacatecas.

The discovery and foundation of Zacatecas were made from Guadalajara. Although the route from Guadalajara to Zacatecas was relatively easy, Spanish authorities realized early on that they needed a more direct route south from Zacatecas. By 1550, only two years after the founding of Zacatecas, construction was under way on the new camino. Some of the proposed route was easy going, but in several locations, substantial work had to be accomplished, especially as the newer and larger *carros* began to supplement small *carretas*.

Problems quickly arose as a direct result of the increasing number of attacks by Chichimeca Indian tribes, whose territory was encroached on by the new camino. The most troublesome were the Guachichiles, who in 1554 attacked sixty wagons with an armed escort near present-day Ojuelos. The Indians took thirty thousand pesos' worth of clothing, silver, and mules.

In an attempt to protect the caravans, the Spanish built fortified towns and small presidios along the camino. The first town in Chichimeca territory on the silver road was San Miguel el Grande (now the town of San Miguel Allende), sited as an Indian town in the 1540s, abandoned in 1551 as a result of attacks, and finally resettled in 1555 on orders from Viceroy Luís de Velasco, this time as a Spanish town. Later (1561), San Felipe de los Reyes was settled north of San Miguel on the camino. Five smaller presidios were constructed at almost equally spaced intervals between San Felipe and Zacatecas. The war between Spaniards and Indians proved to be serious, lasting from 1550 to about 1600.

But the presidio system worked no better in the sixteenth century than it would in the eighteenth or nineteenth. Presidios simply meant more horses to steal for the Indians. What brought this war to a close was diplomacy and especially the introduction of sedentary farming Indians from the south, a tactic known

El Camino de la Plata

The silver highway south to Mexico City, El Camino de la Plata, traversed the edge of one of the most aggressive Indian tribes, the Guachichil. The road, as one historian wrote, was the Achillean heel of the wealth in the north. The Indians were fearless, and the Spanish needed a new strategy to deal with the threats posed by this and other tribes. The silver being extracted in Zacatecas and other bonanza sites wasn't helping Spain unless it could be sent south to Mexico City.

The construction of the camino between Zacatecas and Querétaro began in 1550 and was used by carretas and carros by 1552. An earlier route between these two communities passed through Guadalajara, but that route was far longer than the one under construction. Zacatecas needed miners, food, and other supplies, and the new camino allowed these items to move north from central Mexico.

To protect this new camino, the Spanish developed fortified towns and strategically placed presidios, small armed camps. The presidios were made of adobe, small, and almost like castles out of the Middle Ages. Spain, of course, wasn't that long out of the Middle Ages itself. The first five presidios (built between Zacatecas and Ojuelos) were to have six soldiers each and were spaced ten to twenty-five miles apart. It was simply a strategy of defense, not pacification. The goal was to keep the silver moving south. During the entire Chichimeca Wars (1550–1600), thirty presidios were established, each with about fourteen soldiers.

The approach used, however, was successful, for even with so few soldiers the caravans were getting through.

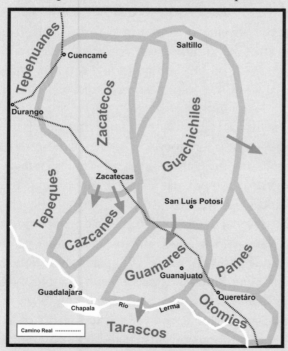

Indian tribes in the Zacatecas area in 1550, based on a map in Philip Wayne Powell's Soldiers, Indians, and Silver: The Northward Advance of New Spain, 1550–1600

Dates and names given by Rivera and Lafora as they traveled
on the Camino de la Plata

Rivera		Lafora	
12/6/1724	Tlacotes	2/11/1768	Tlacotes
12/5/1724	Cienega de Larranaga	2/12/1768	Ciénega Grande
12/4/1724	Ojuelos	2/13/1768	Ojuelos
12/3/1724	Hac. Gachupines	2/14/1768	Villa San Felipe, Hac. Quemada, Hac. Las Tranchas
12/1/1724	Villa San Felipe		
11/30/1724	Hac. Gallinero, Hac. Las Trancas, Hac. Quemada	2/15/1768	Dolores (Hidalgo), Hac. de la R (Erre), Atotonilco, San Miguel
11/29/1724	Hac. de la R (Erre)		
11/27/1724	San Miguel		

Moreover, the impact of the presidios went beyond soldiering. Wives and children of the soldiers accompanied them to their posts, and the safety engendered by the military force encouraged merchants, stockmen, and farmers to cluster near the presidios, many of which became towns.

To trace the route today, we can rely in part on two careful observers who used this route in the eighteenth century. One of them, Pedro de Rivera, was sent to the frontier (all the way to Santa Fé, Sonora, and Texas) in 1724 to inspect defensive posts. The Marqués de Rubí, on another presidio inspection in 1766 to 1768, came south on the Camino de la Plata in 1768. Nicolás de Lafora, Rubí's second in command, kept a journal, on which we will rely. Rivera moved north along the Camino de la Plata, whereas Rubí and Lafora were returning south from their long inspection.

The accompanying table makes clear that Rivera and Lafora are describing the same route. Each mentioned more places than are listed in the table, but only those places listed can be visited today. To find the locations, you are urged to buy the state maps published by Guia Roji, for the other published maps may not have the locations on them. You also can find the locations on the 1:250,000-scale maps published by INEGI, the government map service. (For information on Guia Roji and INEGI, see the appendix.) All of the communities listed in the table are found within a few miles of México 51, the principal highway between Ojuelos and San Miguel Allende.

In addition to the many presidios along this route, two fortified towns, San Felipe and San Miguel (now San Miguel de Allende), were built. Neither Rivera nor Lafora mentions the fortified nature of the route, probably because the Chichimeca Wars were over by 1600 or shortly thereafter, so they were traveling long after hostilities had ended.

Camino de la Plata, north section

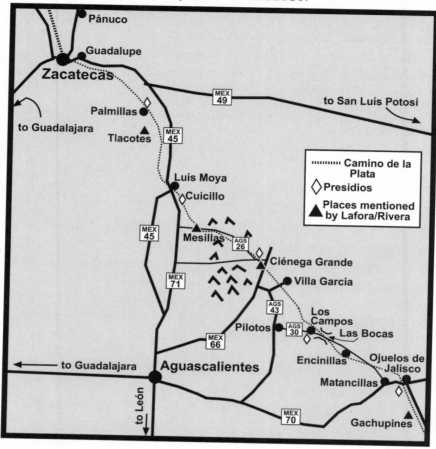

as "peace by purchase." Tlaxcalan Indians in particular came north to farm and work and by example showed the Chichimecas an alternative to warfare.

Depart Zacatecas on México 45. This road passes through the suburb of Guadalupe, an important colonial location. The Convento de Guadalupe, adjacent to the Jardín Juárez, is worth visiting. The convento, established by Franciscan padres in 1708 as a place to prepare the many missionaries who were to head north, includes a colonial museum with numerous angels and saints on display.

From Guadalupe continue on México 45. It will turn south (signs point to Aguascalientes), with México 49 going east to San Luís Potosí. Continue south on 45 to KM marker 93, then just beyond a bus stop, take a road to the right (Rural 321) to Palmillas, six kilometers (3.6 miles) away. A presidio was built at Palmillas in the 1570s, one of the first five presidios established. Situated about six leagues (twenty-four miles) from Zacatecas, it was commonly utilized as a paraje. As you enter the village, what looks like the old camino enters from the left.

Return to México 45, turn right, and go through Ojo Caliente to Luís Moya, where you switch at the south edge of town from México 45 to México 71. In a few kilometers, you come to Cuicillo (at KM 39), one of fifteen additional presidios built in the last decades of the sixteenth century to protect the camino from intensifying Indian attacks. El Coesillo, as it was known then, was built on an important site at the junction where the Camino de la Plata met roads from Aguascalientes and San Luís Potosí. There isn't much to see in Cuicillo today.

CIÉNEGA GRANDE

Continue south on México 71 to the junction with Aguascalientes 26, turn left, and drive toward Delicias and Mesillas. This route was difficult to decipher, but Rivera's mentioning Mesillas in 1724 became the essential clue. When the pavement ends at Mesillas, continue east on a decent gravel road toward Tepetate and Jarillas. At a junction past Jarillas, take the left branch toward San Gil. When you reach pavement at San Gil, turn left to go to the nearby town of Ciénega Grande.

There was a presidio here, one of the original five built in the 1570s. Pedro Rivera passed through here in 1724, as did Nicolás Lafora in 1767, both of them mentioning the town, but the presidio had been extinguished by the time of their visits. No markers are here, but you can see a nice plaza and several churches.

From Ciénega Grande, continue south on México 66 to Aguascalientes 43, where you turn left. A short drive (four kilometers, or 2.4 miles) on 43 brings you to Highway 47, where you turn left toward Villa Garcia (about eight kilometers, or 4.8 miles). You will see another set of three historical markers at the edge of town (three if the one lying on the ground has been replaced). The historian Powell says a presidio lay south and west of here, but it almost certainly was south and east, as you'll see.

Las Bocas de Gallardo

Return to Highway 43 via the same route and turn left on Aguascalientes 43. Continue southeast on this road until you reach the turn for Pilotos (just past KM marker 34, with a Pemex station at the corner). Turn left (east) here on Aguascalientes 30 for Los Campos. The road, paved as far as Los Campos, becomes gravel just east of Los Campos and enters a narrow stretch between mountains, called Las Bocas. The mouth, Las Bocas, is certainly where the presidio Las Bocas was. On the San Miguel map, it is called Las Bocas Con Su Fuerte. The San Miguel map was drawn in the sixteenth century and can be found as the frontispiece in Powell's book. *Fuerte* on the map indicates a presidio, or fort. This opening was often called Las Bocas de Gallardo. The hacienda Gallardo was situated at the present town of Palo Alto, about sixteen kilometers (ten miles) south of Pilotos.

Continue east on the gravel road toward the next community, that of Encinillas, mentioned by almost every traveler. You are now in the state of Jalisco, having entered it just about where you departed from Los Campos. Continue east until you reach the community of Matancillas, where you meet the pavement again at México 70. Turn left here and continue to Ojuelos de Jalisco.

Ojuelos de Jalisco

Both Rivera and Lafora mention Ojuelos (the Jalisco was added later), for each passed through this town. Ojuelos was another of the original five presidios established in about 1570 (it is noted on Powell's San Miguel map) to address the growing Guachuchil threat. That neither Rivera nor Lafora mentioned presidios can be explained by the fact that presidios had long been abandoned when they passed through. When the Chichimeca Wars ended, after 1600, the garrisons were moved farther north, where they were needed.

At the plaza in Ojuelos, turn right on México 80 (the sign will say to Lago de Moreno) and go one block and turn left, following this road out of town. Then, just past some arches over the highway, turn left on México 51 toward Ocampo.

Just after you pass into the state of Guanajuato, you will find a turn to the right for the small town of Gachupines, a town on the Camino de la Plata mentioned by Rivera in 1724. Today Gachupines is a pleasant village with little to remind one of its past. Return to México 51 and turn right.

You will pass through the small city of Ocampo, then, about fifteen kilometers (nine miles) past Ocampo (near km marker 157), you will enter a pass, a *portezuelo*, that had an early presidio. Called El Fuerte today, this place is ideally situated in a pass and near water. This presidio location appears on the famous San Miguel map as Fuerte Del Portezuelo de S. Felipe. The Instituto Nacional de Antropología y Historia (INAH) has placed markers on the highway describing this site.

Continuing south on México 51 brings you to the old fortified town of San Felipe. Founded in 1561, San Felipe was mentioned as a small villa by Lafora and simply called the villa de San Felipe by Rivera. It, too, can be found on the San Miguel map. México 51 continues south and at about 23 kilometers (13.8 miles)

CAMINO DE LA PLATA, SOUTH SECTION

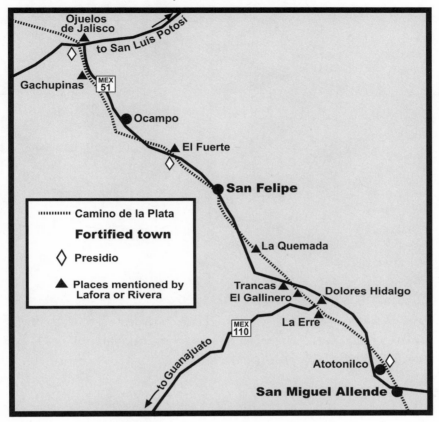

twists and turns a bit where a road to the left leads to Quemada (at about KM 116). Rivera stopped at the hacienda Quemada in 1724, as did Lafora in 1767. This hacienda is still being used and is worth a visit. One can still see the gun slits on the front. Return to México 51 and turn left.

Another 12 kilometers (7.2 miles) on México 51 will take you to another hacienda (Las Trancas) where both Rivera and Lafora passed. Look for the sign Tranza Vieja and drive to the right 1 kilometer (0.6 mile). This hacienda has been restored and is available to rent. The hacienda church is situated on the attractive plaza.

A few miles beyond Las Trancas, look for a road to your right to El Gallinero—actually several roads lead down to this stop on the camino. Gallinero was another hacienda, one mentioned by Rivera in 1724. Today it is still in use as a private home. Return to México 51 and make your way south to Dolores Hidalgo.

*The hacienda of La Erre (written La R by early travelers) is south of
Dolores Hidalgo. A marker can be seen on the wall honoring
a visit by Padre Hidalgo. Photo by author.*

Dolores Hidalgo

The next stop is the small historic city of Dolores Hidalgo, called Dolores in 1767
by Lafora. The addition of *Hidalgo* to the name occurred after the events of 1810,
which have made the town a shrine for Mexico. Instigators of the war of independence from Spain lived in the area between Dolores and Querétaro. Padre
Miguel Hidalgo y Costilla, a parish priest in Dolores, on September 16, 1810, proclaimed Mexican independence in a grito, or proclamation. Although the war
began well for Hidalgo and his fellow conspirators, it soon turned sour. Hidalgo
was captured, imprisoned at Chihuahua (you saw his cell there), and executed.

    The town of Dolores is on the Camino Real, but all sites are Hidalgo ori-
ented. Find the large church downtown where Hidalgo gave his grito. Also
worth seeing is the Museo de la Independencia Nacional, half a block west of the
plaza. The house where Hidalgo and the others did their last-minute plotting is
one block south of the plaza.

The next stop, another old hacienda mentioned by Lafora and Rivera, is Hacienda de la Erre. It is well worth the few extra miles you will drive to get there. Leave Dolores Hidalgo on México 110, the highway to Guanajuato. At about KM marker 7, you will pass over the Río de la Erre, and just beyond is a road to the left for La Erre (there is no sign). Drive down this road about one mile and you will see the old hacienda to the left and, next to it, a church. On the building, a marker recognizes a visit by Padre Hidalgo on his way south to fight the Spaniards. Return to Dolores Hidalgo and look for México 51, which will take you to San Miguel de Allende.

At a point just beyond KM 66, turn off the highway to the village of Atotonilco ("hot water" in Nahuatl). The camino passed through the village on its way to La Erre. Toward the end of the Chichimeca Wars, in 1590, a presidio had to be established at Atotonilco, but it was abandoned in 1607. The modern village has a nice sanctuary, Santuario de Atotonilco, and is the goal of many pilgrimages.

SAN MIGUEL DE ALLENDE

Return to México 51 and continue to San Miguel de Allende. México 51 enters town and becomes Hidalgo, which leads directly to the plaza principal, or *jardín*. San Miguel el Grande, its colonial name, was founded first as an Indian town in the 1540s. It had to be abandoned in 1551 because of Indian raids but was reestablished as a Spanish town in 1555 by Viceroy Velasco. It was meant to be a fortified town, but this never came to pass. It became secure when sufficient settlers arrived in the area and especially after San Felipe de los Reyes was established north of here in 1561.

The name used today, San Miguel de Allende, is a result of the town's being the birthplace of Ignacio Allende, one of Hidalgo's fellow conspirators. A major destination of both expatriates and tourists, the city produces a weekly English-language newspaper called *Atención San Miguel*. It has many hotels, restaurants, and other places of interest to tourists.

La Parroquia de San Miguel Arcángel, on the south side of the plaza principal, dates from the seventeenth century. Its towers were a late-nineteenth-century addition. The church on the left, Iglesia San Rafael, was built in 1742. Although readers of this guide are likely to loiter in this lovely town for several days, there is little of camino interest here.

Leave San Miguel on México 111 for Querétaro. To find this road, drive east on San Francisco, then right on Vargas, heading out of the basin and on toward Querétaro.

QUERÉTARO

Entering Querétaro, look for the signs to Centro. This city of half a million residents was very important for the Camino Real. It was, for centuries, the last city before the frontier began. Beyond Querétaro, towns, cities, and presidios were but stepping-stones in a great *despoblado*, unoccupied zone. And somewhat paradoxically, the city that trained missionaries to help conquer New Mexico, Texas, and California couldn't conquer its own Sierra Gorda, a part of Querétaro state, occupied by resisting Pamé Indians.

Querétaro was the city of convents on the barbarian frontier. The Otomí Indians moved into the area in the fifteenth century, only to be absorbed into the Aztec empire in the early sixteenth. On June 25, 1531, a battle took place in Querétaro between some Christianized Otomís and Spaniards on one side and "infidel" Otomís and perhaps some Chichimecas on the other. The story goes that St. James, Santiago, appeared in the sky during an eclipse, winning the day for the Christians. Querétaro is truly a colonial gem and should be savored during your visit.

The Camino Real followed today's Corregidora, which passes by the plaza principal, or Jardín Zenea as it is called (A on the accompanying map). From the plaza, the camino descended to the river, passing almost immediately into the land of the Chichimecas. Start at the plaza, cross Corregidora and turn right for the 1660 Templo de San Francisco (B). This temple sits on the place where the original convent was built in 1548. Next to the *templo*, to its right, is the Museo Regional de Querétaro, housed in part of the monastery and seminary that made up the Templo de San Francisco complex. The museum contains the table at which the Treaty of Guadalupe Hidalgo was signed, ending the war between the United States and Mexico in 1848.

Leaving the plaza, walk north two blocks to Morelos, turn left, and go one block to the Convento del Carmen (C). This church was constructed in 1618. Next continue west on Morelos to Allende, turn left, and walk three blocks to Madero. On the corner of Madero and Allende stands the Iglesia de Santa Clara (D). Construction started on this church in 1607, and it was one of the richest convents in New Spain.

Now return to the Jardín Zenea. Go east on 5 de Mayo a few blocks until you see V. Carranza entering at an angle from your right. Take Carranza, going up a slight hill to arrive at the Plaza de los Fundadores (E). This hilltop plaza marks the spot on which the battle for Querétaro was fought in June 1531. The beautiful church on the plaza is the Convento de la Santa Cruz de Milagros.

QUERÉTARO

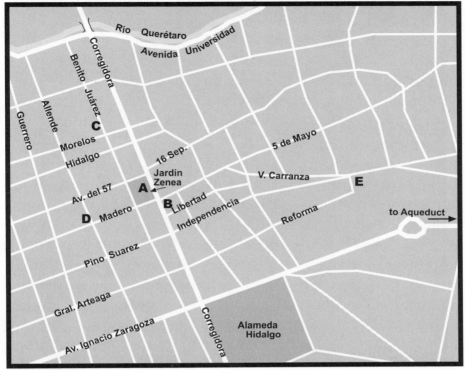

KEY
A Jardín Zenea
B Templo de San Francisco
C Convento del Carmen
D Iglesia de Santa Clara
E Plaza de Fundadores

Although the original convent was begun here in 1531, the present convento probably dates from the seventeenth century. Serving as Maximilian's headquarters from March 13 to May 15, 1867, during the battle for Querétaro, it became his prison when he was captured after the battle and later shot.

Two more locations in the city are worth visiting. The aqueduct, begun in 1726 and finished in 1738, still supplies water to the city. To see this 12-kilometer (7.2-mile) marvel, walk east on Zaragoza about half a kilometer from the Plaza de los Fundadores. To reach the other location of interest, in the western portion of the city, you will want to use your car. The Parque Municipal Cerro de las Campanas is off Avenida Universidad, which parallels the river. Drive west on Universidad to the park, where Maximilian was executed and his family (he was

San Miguel to Mexico City

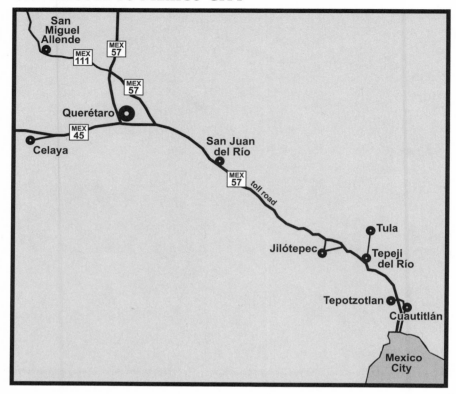

a Hapsburg) has since erected a chapel in his memory. You will also find a museum featuring the siege of Querétaro, the battle between the royalist forces of Maximilian and the Mexicans.

Leaving Querétaro, look for the signs to Mexico City, México 57, on the toll road, or *cuota*. The toll booth isn't reached until you arrive at the Querétaro-Hidalgo state boundary. The present toll road between Querétaro and the capital is never very far from the old Camino Real. Two towns will be featured on your way to Mexico City, San Juan del Río and Tepeji del Río.

On México 57, look for the signs to San Juan del Río at approximately 52 kilometers (31.2 miles). Follow the highway toward the city center on México 57, and continue to the exit for Tepeji del Río. When you cross the river, the bridge you use is called Puente de la Venta. Constructed in 1710, it still carries motor traffic today. This is the same bridge that would have carried camino traffic after 1710. The city itself was founded in the same year as Querétaro, 1531. Continuing on Avenida

Juárez, you pass by on your left the Hospital de San Juan de Dios, built in 1661. Farther along on Avenida Juárez, you come to the beautiful white Convento de Santo Domingo, constructed in about 1691.

Return to the toll road by going in the direction of La Murella and Amealco, which will take you to a second San Juan del Río exit. Or you can return the way you came, but if you choose this route, you must turn back toward Querétaro and do a U-turn at Loma Linda, thus heading once again toward Mexico City.

Once you are back on México 57, continue to the exit for Tepeji del Río. This is also an exit for Tula de Allende, an important archaeological zone since it was the Toltec capital. Drive into Tepeji and then return to the toll road. There isn't much to see. Tepeji was on the camino, as noted by Nicolás Lafora (he called it Tepexe del Río) in March 1766.

The last toll booth is near the town of Tepotzotlan in the state of Mexico. Both Lafora and Pedro Rivera mention this town, a very early colonial town likely settled by 1530. It is worth visiting, either now or when you leave Mexico City as you return north. The last town outside the capital and on the Camino Real is Cuautitlán. This community is now completely absorbed by Mexico City and is hardly worth a visit. If you want to see it, take the road to Cuautitlán, about five kilometers (three miles) east of the main road and about five kilometers from Tepotzotlan.

Continue south, entering Mexico City.

✝ ✝ ✝

CHAPTER SEVEN
Mexico City

✝ ✝ ✝

TENOCHTITLÁN

When Hernán Cortés and his force arrived at the present-day site of Mexico City in November 1519, there were two occupied islands, Tenochtitlán and Tlatelolco, in a large, shallow lake. The population on the islands was approximately two hundred thousand, which, for the sixteenth century, made the Aztec capital a very large city, whether in the New or Old World. Causeways connecting the islands to the lake's edge provided for land movement, and additionally, the lake itself was used for transport by canoes.

The two islands of Tenochtitlán and Tlatelolco are easily picked out on the map. The dotted lines going west and south from Tenochtitlán were causeways, now called *calzadas,* along which were bridged openings. Bernal Diaz, a soldier in Cortés's party, noted these causeways:

> During the morning, we arrived at a broad Causeway and
> continued our march towards Iztapalapa, and when we saw so
> many cities and villages built in the water and other great towns
> on dry land and that straight and level Causeway going towards
> Mexico, we were amazed and said that it was like the enchantments
> they tell of in the Legend of Amadis. . . .

TENOCHTITLÁN, THE AZTEC CAPITAL

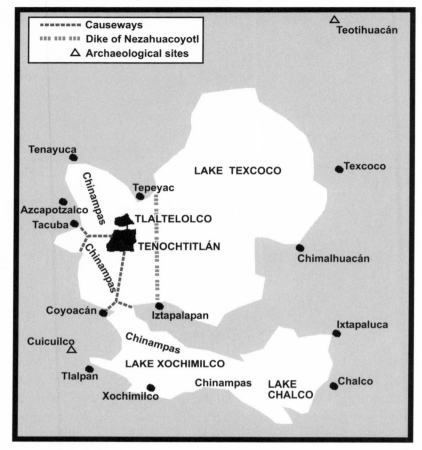

Two archaeological zones are indicated on the map: Teotihuacán and Cuicuilco. Both had been deserted or, in the case of Cuicuilco, destroyed by volcanic eruption for centuries before the Aztecs arrived in the Valley of Mexico. A north-south line just east of Tenochtitlán represents the Dike of Nezahuacoyotl, built to keep the western portion of the lake filled with fresh, not saline, water. Because the mountains to the west of the valley receive more precipitation, the runoff kept the western portion of the lake fresher. *Chinampas* (raised fields) crowded the western and southern shores of the lake. These chinampas provided the food for the many residents of the Aztec capital. There were many towns around the lake, but only a few of these are shown and named. They are today all active communities in the Mexico City urban area.

*Model of Aztec Tenochtitlán before the conquest. It is adjacent
to the cathedral. Photo by author.*

At the time of the Spanish entrada, the two cities Tenochtitlán and Tlatelolco
were considerably more populous than London, which had but fifty thousand
residents. Feeding an urban population was always a great challenge, but the chinampa system was so efficient that it supported the very large urban population at
Tenochtitlán. Soldiers with Cortés, many of whom had visited large European
cities of the time, were astounded at the size of the city.

The Aztecs had arrived in central Mexico in the middle of the thirteenth
century, having come from the north as another in a series of Chichimec inva-
sions. In their short time in central Mexico, they conquered almost all of the local
Indian nations. One significant exception to their domination was the area
known as Tlaxcala. (Today the Mexican state of Tlaxcala is to the east of Mexico
City.) The Tlaxcalans, who for whatever reason had not been subdued, subsequently became allies of the Spanish when they arrived and contributed signifi-
cantly to the eventual Spanish military victory over the Aztecs at Tenochtitlán.
This alliance between Spaniard and Tlaxcalan persisted, with some Tlaxcalans
migrating north with the Spaniards into Zacatecas and New Mexico. The Spanish

found them to be dependable settlers who could teach the Chichimecs agricultural practices.

Food for this large urban population was produced at the edge of the lake in "raised gardens," or chinampas as they are called, built of reeds and mud from the lake and irrigated naturally from the adjacent canals, with water moving horizontally through the chinampas. Canals were left between the gardens for irrigation so that the produce of corn, beans, tomatoes, and squash could be easily transported to the markets in Tenochtitlán and Tlatelolco by canoe. At least two crops per year could be harvested from these gardens. The Floating Gardens of Xochimilco south of Mexico City are surviving examples of this extraordinarily productive agricultural system. The natives of Mexico had no animals that could pull wagons or carts, due to the lack of wild animals suitable for such domestication. The chinampa system solved the food production problem and the canals solved the transportation problem, allowing a large city to grow and prosper.

Cortés and his men stayed in Tenochtitlán until June 1520, when they were expelled by the Aztecs. At night Cortés, the Spaniards, and their Indian allies made their way on the causeway toward Tacuba. This retreat was known as the Noche de Triste, "Night of Sadness," for the Spaniards. Cortés, it is said, wept bitterly under a tree along the causeway known as the Árbol de la Noche Triste. This very causeway—many of the Aztec causeways became roads and are called calzadas today—became the principal road to Querétaro, Zacatecas, and the north as the Camino Real de Tierra Adentro.

In May 1521, Cortés returned and conquered the city. Ostensibly the conquest resulted from force of arms, but Cortés's mysterious ally, his fifth column, was smallpox. Smallpox (and other diseases such as measles and typhus) were Old World diseases for which the native population of the New World had no resistance. It was smallpox that decimated the Aztec army many times over and opened the way for eventual Spanish occupation. Smallpox epidemics seemed to pulse through Mexico at 10 to 15-year intervals, reducing a precontact population in the central highlands of Mexico of 15 million to 1.8 million by 1605.

ZÓCALO (CONSTITUTION SQUARE)

The focal point of the Aztec capital, the templo mayór, was the area that now lies under and around the zócalo, the principal plaza in Mexico City. The Spanish destroyed the Aztec capital to build theirs on its remains. Slowly the Spanish city expanded until construction was accomplished on the two islands and even encroached on the old lake bed. The lake today has mostly disappeared, but evidence

MEXICO CITY

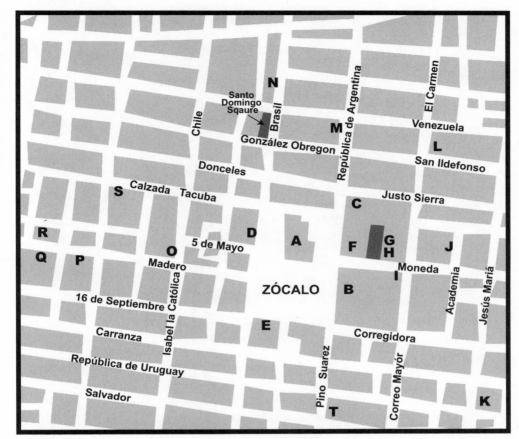

KEY

A Cathedral	**L** San Pedro y San Pablo Church
B National Palace	**M** La Encarnacíon Convent
C Templo Mayór	**N** Santo Domingo Church
D Monte de Piedad	**O** La Profesa Church
E Old Town Hall	**P** Iturbide Palace
F Ex-Archbishopric Palace	**Q** San Francisco Church
G Santa Teresa la Antigua	and Ex-convento
H First Printing House	**R** House of Tiles
I The Mint	**S** Santa Clara Church
J Ex-Santa Inés Convent	**T** Mexico City Museum
K La Merced Cloister	

The cathedral and zócalo in Mexico City. This site is where the
very center of Aztec Tenochtitlán was situated. Photo by author.

of its location can sometimes be ascertained by noting buildings far below street
level or tilted due to uneven subsidence.

A sense of the original Spanish city exists if one seeks it out. Many colonial
buildings can be visited in the historic central district, and the street pattern in this
district is, of course, colonial. Today the hustle and bustle of Mexico City, with
almost twenty million residents, makes it challenging to get around and see every-
thing. Most sites that you will be directed to are an easy walk from the zócalo.

This immense square owes its name to a plan, never fulfilled, for a large column to be built on a base, a zócalo. The base was finished at one time, hence the
name *zócalo*, but the column was not forthcoming. The Metropolitan Cathedral
stands on one side of this plaza, the National Palace on another, and the town hall
on yet another. The plaza is filled with thousands of citizens every September 15,
when, at eleven o'clock at night, the president recites the grito, or call for independence, first spoken by Father Hidalgo in Dolores in 1810. It is a very important
and symbolic location for Mexico. Starting at the zócalo, you will find the following sites not too far away.

Metropolitan Cathedral (on the Zócalo)

This is an unusual church (A on the map) because, in part, of its drawn-out construction. Begun in 1573, the church's foundation alone took forty-two years to lay. The rest of the church was built between 1615 and 1813. Therefore, as a result of this long period, the church incorporates many architectural styles.

National Palace (on the Zócalo)

The building (B) was actually the residence of Hernán Cortés at one time. Countless modifications have been made through the centuries. The balcony above the central doorway is the one from which the president gives the grito each September 15. Inside the palace, you will see numerous works by the prominent Mexican muralist Diego Rivera. The mural *Present and Future Mexico* contains a "who's who" of history, including images of Rockefeller and Frida Kahlo, that can be picked out with careful observation.

Templo Mayór (Behind the Cathedral)

Behind and east of the cathedral stands one small part of the Aztec temple, the Templo Mayór (C). Spanish chroniclers state the original temple was 500 meters (1,650 feet) long and contained 78 buildings. As you pass through the site on metal walkways, you can get a sense of what greeted Cortés and his retinue in 1519.

Monte de Piedad (West of the Cathedral)

This building (D) was once part of the estate owned by Hernán Cortés. The original structure during Cortés's residence was bounded by today's Madero, Isabel de Católica, Tacuba, and Monte de Piedad streets. Today it is the national pawnshop and has been since 1836. Every two weeks, unclaimed objects are sold here in public auction. Go inside to see the vast collection of "stuff."

Old Town Hall (on the South Side of the Zócalo)

As in almost every planned Spanish New World city, the *ayuntamiento*, or town hall, is across the plaza from the principal church (E). The original structure was built in the sixteenth century and burned during the food riots in the seventeenth. It was rebuilt in 1720.

Ex-Archbishopric Palace (4 Moneda)

Across from the northwest corner of the National Palace is the Ex-Archbishopric Palace, built beginning immediately after the conquest (F). The archdiocese included all of New Spain and the Philippines at that time. It is now a museum and worth visiting.

Santa Teresa la Antigua (6 Licenciado Primo de Verdad)

This cloister was consecrated in 1684 and rebuilt in 1798 and again in 1813. It collapsed during an earthquake in 1845 but was rebuilt once more (G).

First Printing House
(Corner of Moneda and Licenciado Primo Verdad)

The first New World printing using movable Gutenberg type was accomplished in this building in 1536. The books printed here were catechisms and other religious tracts. It is now an exhibition center with a bookstore (H).

The Mint (13 Moneda)

The mint (I), whose construction was begun in 1570 as part of the viceregal palace, had fallen into ruin by 1667, when repairs were made. It was remodeled again in 1729 as a result of a renewed flow of silver from the mines. It is now the Cultural Museum.

Ex–Santa Inés Convent (13 Academia)

This cloister was built in 1600 and intended to house thirty-three nuns, the number of years Christ lived (J). It is now the José Luís Cuevas Museum.

La Merced Cloister (170 República de Uruguay)

This cloister, begun in 1602 and completed toward the end of the century, is very unusual because of its Moorish style. It is now a National Fine Arts Institute tapestry workshop (K).

San Pedro y San Pablo Church
(Corner of El Carmen and San Ildefonso)

This is a Jesuit church begun in 1574 and under Jesuit control until the brothers were expelled from the New World in 1767. It is now the Museum of Light (L).

La Encarnación Convent (28 República de Argentina)

This convent was founded in 1594 (M). The temple was started in 1639 and consecrated in 1645. Diego Rivera painted 235 panels in the building between 1923 and 1928. This building is an icon of sorts for Mexican painters and well worth a visit for its architecture and Rivera work.

Santo Domingo Church in Mexico City. Photo by author.

Santo Domingo Church
(Santo Domingo Square)

All that is left of the original church is seen on the one side of the square in front of the larger church. The first church dates from the period immediately after the conquest. A second church, now gone, was built here between 1556 and 1571. The present church, the third, was begun in 1717 (N).

La Profesa Church
(Madero and Isabel la Católica)

The Jesuits established a house for monks here in 1578, which led to disagreements with the other orders (O). The Jesuits prevailed, however, and constructed this church in 1597–1610. The original church had to be rebuilt as a result of floods in 1629. This latest version, with a few parts of the earlier, was built in 1720.

Iturbide Palace (17 Madero)

Iturbide, the first president after the Spanish were defeated, never owned this palace but did stay here for a while (P). Built in the late eighteenth century, it remains a beautiful example of a home of the very wealthy in this period. Today the palace is owned by Banamex Cultural Foundation and holds short-term exhibitions.

San Francisco Church and Ex-Convento (7 Madero)

The Franciscans were the first religious order on the scene at the time of the conquest. The church you see today at 7 Madero was built in 1710 (Q), since its predecessors at this site had sunk. The area you are now in was not on the island of the Aztecs but rather on the old lake bed. Because the lake bed has been filled but improperly compacted, as the city has grown, buildings constructed on it tend to either sink or tilt. The church you see at 7 Madero started at street level in 1710, when it was built. The Franciscan convent extended many blocks from the present church.

House of Tiles (4 Madero)

Now a Sanborns restaurant, the House of Tiles, or Casa de Azulejos, is a real gem (R). The building was constructed in 1737 and covered with tiles from Puebla. The feeling inside is of Mudejar, the term used to describe the Moorish characteristics brought to New World architecture. A mural found at the first landing titled *Omniscience* is by José Clemente Orozco, another famous Mexican muralist.

Santa Clara Church (29 Calzada Tacuba)

This church was finished by 1661. It belonged to the Poor Clare nuns, but after secularization, it was used for many purposes, including grocery store and cantina. It is now the Mexican Congress Library (S).

Mexico City Museum (30 Pino Suarez)

This building, on top of the Aztec Iztapalapa causeway, is one of the oldest in Mexico (T). At the corner of the building, note the beautiful stone serpent's head that serves as cornerstone. This likely came from the Templo Mayór after it was destroyed. The museum has extensive displays on the history of the city.

Note that the street behind the cathedral is named Tacuba, or Calzada Tacuba. This is the route of the Camino Real as it approached the zócalo. Silver from Zacatecas or other northern mining communities went directly to the mint, located barely one block off the zócalo. You may recall that in Zacatecas

At the corner of the Museum of Mexico City is this interesting cornerstone. It came from the Aztec Plaza Mayór. Photo by author

the road leading south, down the arroyo, was and is called Calle Tacuba. That was the silver road. There were Tacuba streets in other camino towns, each being the road to Tacuba and Mexico City.

Several other locations in the city will interest camino followers. Continuing west on Tacuba (it will change names several times) takes you past the large urban park Alameda. A block past the Alameda, Tacuba (now Hidalgo) intersects Paseo de la Reforma.

This is the spot where the five young cadets jumped to their death rather than surrender to American forces in 1847. Chapultepec Castle is in the background. Photo by author.

CHAPULTEPEC PARK

Turning left, southwest, on Paseo de la Reforma will lead you to Chapultepec Park. Reforma itself is an interesting French-style boulevard. Much of late-nineteenth-century Mexico City was inspired by French models. Continuing southwest on Reforma takes you through a very modern commercial section of the capital.

Once you enter Chapultepec Park, you may see Chapultepec Castle (if the smog isn't too bad) to the left. The castle was partly built in 1785 as residence for the viceroys. In 1843 it was converted into a military academy, and later it became the residence of Emperor Maximilian and Empress Carlotta. It served as the residence of Mexican presidents until 1940, when President Lázaro Cárdenas

TACUBA TO THE ZÓCALO

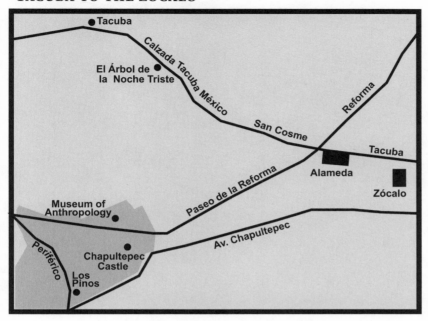

moved to new quarters and made it the Museo Nacional de Historia. In 1848 the hill was the site of one of the last battles of the war between Mexico and the United States. It was defended in part by the young cadets of the military academy. These were the "Niños Heroes," child heroes, for whom streets are named all through the republic.

Also in the park is the extraordinary Museum of Anthropology. You will find it on the right about 1 kilometer (0.6 mile) after entering the park. The museum houses examples of artifacts from every Indian nation in Mexico, prehistoric as well as historic. A section on the ground floor displays the earliest artifacts, including tiny, two-inch corn cobs found in caves in the Tehuacan Valley. Corn was domesticated in or near that valley some six thousand years ago.

Also in the park, you can see Los Pinos, the Mexican White House, and nearby is Molina del Rey, site of another major Mexican War battle.

ÁRBOL DE LA NOCHE TRISTE

On your way north out of the city, you should follow Calzada Tacuba, since it sits on the Camino Real. Look carefully for a tiny park or fenced area on the left where the Árbol de la Noche Triste is situated. This is supposedly the tree

This stump is all that remains of the Árbol de la Noche Triste, the tree of the sad night. This is supposedly the tree under which Cortes wept as he left Tenochtitlán. Photo by author.

(now a tree stump) where Cortés wept on leaving Tenochtitlán. He was probably weeping as a result of losing all the gold left behind.

Continue past the community of Tacuba and join the periférico leading north toward Querétaro.

CHAPTER EIGHT

Guanajuato and North

✝   ✝   ✝

The return north will follow a later version of the Camino Real. From Mexico City to Querétaro, you will take the same route you followed south, but from Querétaro, the later camino passed west and then north through the Bajío, a very rich agricultural region today, on its way to Zacatecas. North of Zacatecas, at Fresnillo, the newer route went due north to Cuencamé, in the state of Durango. North of Cuencamé, you will be on the camino that was used from the outset as far north as southern Chihuahua state. From Guajoquilla, present-day Ciudad Jiménez, the later route followed the Río Florido, then the Río Conchos to Chihuahua.

A very good description of the region around Querétaro is provided by George Ruxton. Passing through this area in 1846, he comments on mundane items such as *pulque*, a mildly intoxicating beverage that was his drink of choice, his *licór divino*, as he called it. Querétaro was the center of the production of pulque, which is made from one of the many varieties of agave or maguey (cactuslike plants). The juice from the plant was gathered daily and fermented and then consumed fresh. Ruxton also mentioned *calinche*, a drink made from the *tunas* (fruit) of cactus.

Ruxton had wanted to remain in Querétaro for some time, but he found when he arrived that the town was filled with soldiers on their way north to San Luís Potosí to fight the American invaders. He ended up leaving soon after arriving.

Querétaro to Zacatecas

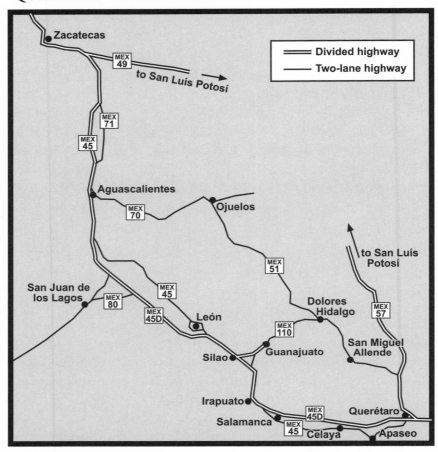

Leave Querétaro on the nontoll road west toward Celaya. The old road dips a little south and passes through Apaseo. Lafora, who stayed here in 1766, called it San Juan Bautista de Apaseo. Ruxton also commented that the houses here that sold pulque had a maguey leaf hung by the door as a sign.

CELAYA

From Apaseo, continue west toward Celaya. Just before you reach the town, you will come to the Río Laja. There is a new bridge over the river here, but if you pass over the bridge, turn immediately right, and pass back over the old bridge, you will see the old camino coming toward you. It was this older bridge that

George Ruxton mentioned the bridge in Celaya on which an inscription honored travelers. This is what is left of that bridge—the inscription is still visible. Photo by author.

Ruxton commented on when he noted that there was an inscription on the abutment that said: *Por el beneficio de los viageros.* The town dwellers built the bridge for the benefit of travelers. You can still see this inscription on an abutment at the north end of the old bridge—it is in the space between the new road and the old.

Celaya, like most of the other towns along this route, was founded in the late sixteenth century. This was in the frontier zone, a zone where sedentary Otomí Indians were farming, but the Chichimecas were a constant threat from the north. Passing through Celaya, you have your choice of routes. You can stay on the Camino Real until reaching Silao, where you will likely turn north to visit Guanajuato, or you can drive directly to Guanajuato from here. If you continue to Silao, you will pass through another camino town, Salamanca. At Silao a toll road will take you to Guanajuato, the state capital.

GUANAJUATO

Guanajuato has become one of Mexico's biggest tourist attractions, and with good reason. It is a beautiful colonial city that has kept most of its charm intact. Silver was discovered here in 1559, and Guanajuato went on to rival Zacatecas in silver output. To enter the city, you should take the road leading into a tunnel that goes under it. When you reach the end of the tunnel (built on the bed of the old Río Guanajuato), surface and then progress down the city. Your first stop should be the tourist office near the main church and plaza unless you already have a good guidebook.

Silver from the mines here was sent east to Dolores (now Dolores Hidalgo), where the Camino Real passed connecting Zacatecas and Mexico City. You can visit the most important mine, La Valenciana, which is still operating today.

Guanajuato was the site of the first major battle during the War of Independence. In 1810, Padre Hidalgo attacked the Spanish force here with twenty thousand men. The Spanish were holed up in the Alhóndiga de Granaditas (granary warehouse). Hidalgo's force entered the building and killed almost every Spaniard inside. Later, the war did not go well for Hidalgo, as he was captured and later executed in Chihuahua. The heads of Hidalgo and his fellow conspirators Aldana, Allende, and Jiménez were placed in cages at the four corners of the Alhóndiga. You can visit the granary, which is now a museum.

Return to Silao and rejoin the toll road toward León. Nicolás Lafora, in 1766, came north and west from Celaya to León, mentioning Salamanca, San José Temascatio, Lo de Sierra, and La Calera, towns that today's traveler passes right by on the way between Celaya and León. Ruxton and Lafora both mention stopping in Silao and León.

SAN JUAN DE LOS LAGOS

Beyond León, Lafora mentioned Lagunillas, whereas Ruxton passed through Lagos de Moreno and Encarnación. The latter two towns are in the state of Jalisco, on the old highway, México 45. At Lagos de Moreno, you can leave the camino and drive west forty-five kilometers (twenty-seven miles) to San Juan de los Lagos, where an annual fair was held the first twelve days in December. Pilgrims had begun coming here in about 1623, and the fair evolved out of those annual visits. By 1797 the fair was well established, and in 1846, when James Josiah Webb visited it, he claimed that fifty thousand to seventy thousand people were in attendance each day.

Webb went on to state that when he visited the fair, he noted pack trains from Monterrey, Tampico, Vera Cruz, and Mazatlán. He said that in one day, some three thousand pack mules arrived from Mazatlán. He also mentioned that a German ship had arrived at San Blas (another west coast port) and sent goods to the fair. The fair was an attraction because no interstate taxes had to be paid. This fair was well known in New Mexico at the time, and caravans were sent south to take advantage of the fair's opportunities. From San Juan de los Lagos, it is an easy return to the camino by way of Encarnación, where you can pick up the toll road again, heading to Aguascalientes.

Aguascalientes was a major stop on this route of the camino. Founded in 1575, it was made a villa in 1611 and a city in 1824 under Mexico. Gregg, who stayed in Aguascalientes in 1835, estimated that its population was about twenty thousand at the time. He said it was beautifully situated on a plain. He visited the warm springs (ojos calientes) for which the town and state were named.

Leave Aguascalientes on the toll road toward Zacatecas. At about thirty kilometers (eighteen miles), you pass by the exit for Pabellón de Arteaga, which Lafora mentioned, and cross into the state of Zacatecas, where you will see an exit for San Pedro, Lafora's last stop before Zacatecas. Although the usual route here would have taken travelers to Cuicillo, since that is where the roads from Aguascalientes and San Miguel met, neither Lafora nor Ruxton mentions Cuicillo. The presidio there had long been extinguished, so it may not have been important enough to mention. Lafora did mention Palmillas, a presidio town you visited on your way south. You have come full circle now and will remain on the camino to Zacatecas.

The route description will begin again at Fresnillos west of Zacatecas, where the later camino went straight north to Cuencamé.

Leave Zacatecas on México 45, the toll road leading toward Fresnillo. Ruxton, in 1846, commented that he saw no inhabitants between Zacatecas and Fresnillo. He encountered a wagon filled with bars of silver headed to the mint at Zacatecas. The wagon was escorted by a heavily armed group of men, all of whom were, as Ruxton said, "galloping at their utmost speed." This stretch of the camino was infested with bands of robbers at the time, and caravans traveled at great risk. Between Fresnillo and Durango, it was the Comanches that travelers had to watch for. Ruxton commented on their raids, too.

Fresnillo, Ruxton found, was a "paltry dirty town." The mines were administered by an American, and many of the miners were Cornish. Ruxton didn't think much of the Cornish miners, who drank and fought constantly. Since Ruxton went on to Durango after his Fresnillo visit, we'll pick up his observations later.

Río Nazas

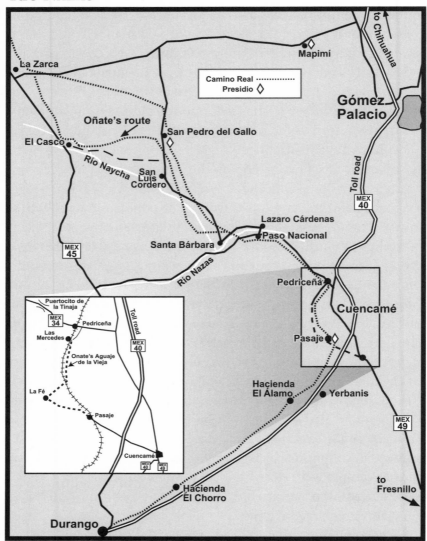

By the late 1830s, the main road, according to Josiah Gregg, went from Fresnillo to Cuencamé without passing through Durango. Therefore, on your trip north, leave Fresnillo on México 45/49 but turn right (north) on 49, about ten kilometers (six miles) past Fresnillo. México 49 will take you directly to Cuencamé through a despoblado, or lightly occupied zone. Only two towns of any consequence are along this 200-kilometer (120-mile) stretch, Rio Grande and Juan Aldama. Aldama, by the way, was one of the four conspirators shot by the Spaniards at Chihuahua, and his was one of the heads hung from the building in Guanajuato.

Cuencamé was first established as a convent in 1589, just a few kilometers southeast of the already-established Camino Real. Gregg called it the "village of churches," for it had five or six such enterprises when he visited in 1839. The Parroquia de San Antonio de Padua, situated on the principal plaza, was built in the late sixteenth century just after the town siting.

PASAJE

From Cuencamé, look for signs to the west for Pasaje. The street to take is called González Ortea, but it may be hard to find. When you arrive at Pasaje, you are back on the old Camino Real. The full name was La Limpia Concepción de Pasaje, and it was established as a presidio in 1685. The Pueblo Revolt in New Mexico in 1680 had become the Great Northern Revolt, with a chain reaction moving southward from tribe to tribe. Recall that the presidio at El Paso del Norte was established in 1683 as a reaction to the spreading revolts. The presidios of San Pedro del Gallo (just north of Pasaje) and San Francisco de Conchos were also established at that time, in 1685.

As usual, look for the church on entering Pasaje. Park nearby and walk around the plaza. Compare the town today with the Urrutia map, and you'll note the church, plaza, and three springs. Walk to the area adjacent to the plaza with the very large trees and look for the spring among the trees. It is somewhat amazing how little the community has changed since Rubí and Urrutia visited it.

When Rubí visited Pasaje in his inspection tour in 1766, Lafora noted the presidial company had a captain, lieutenant, sergeant, and thirty-three soldiers. What set this presidio apart was that it was privately funded. It was situated on land owned by the Conde de San Pedro del Álamo, who also provided the funds to maintain it. Lafora was not impressed with the work being accomplished at the presidio. He thought that it should be abandoned, "otherwise it will probably end in ruining the Count of San Pedro del Álamo, at whose expense it exists." The presidio had been manned by ten armed men from 1743 onward. In 1751 an order had come to increase the force at Pasaje to thirty-three, the number recorded by Lafora.

The camino from Durango to Pasaje passed through El Chorro (still a spot on the map) and Hacienda El Álamo. The hacienda was likely on El Álamo arroyo, which leads from Jesús Agustín Castro, a town south of Yerbanis. Following,

Water cypresses in the center of Pasaje. These trees are watered by the same springs that Urrutia located on his map of 1767. Photo by author.

more or less, the present highway from Durango to Cuencamé, the camino turned northwest toward Pasaje a few kilometers north of Yerbanis. It passed through "Puerto los Carros" before meeting up with today's railroad south of Pasaje.

Leaving Pasaje, drive northwest on a good gravel road toward La Fé. You may have to ask someone for directions to La Fé. When you reach La Fé, turn right and head back toward the railroad. In a few miles, you pass the tracks and the road turns left to follow them. You are back on the camino, following the railroad tracks now, and you reach the pavement again at Las Mercedes. Las

PLAN OF THE PRESIDIO OF PASAJE

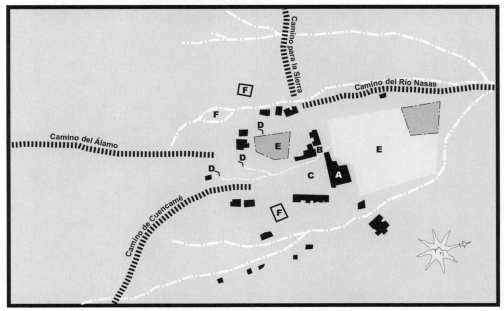

Based on a map drawn by Joseph de Urrutia in 1766

KEY

A House of the Captain
   and guardhouse

B Church

C Plaza

D Several springs

E Captain's vegetable
   garden and orchard

F Corrals for cattle

Mercedes is situated where Oñate's journal had Aguaje de la Vieja (*aguaje* is a watering hole). A small hamlet you passed just before reaching Las Mercedes is still called La Vieja. Here the first water was available since travelers left Pasaje.

Continuing north on the pavement takes you to Pedriceña. The only trail traveler to mention the latter town was Ruxton, who misspelled it as Perdizenia. Neither Lafora nor Rivera mentions this site but instead both say that the next stop north of Pasaje was at La Tinaja (water jug). When you arrive at Pedriceña, go left on México 34 toward Nazas and Paso Nacional. In a few kilometers (KM marker 14), you pass through an opening between two mountainous areas. This is likely the Puertocito de la Tinaja, the location that Lafora and Rivera mentioned. Continue north, where you will descend into the valley of the Río Nazas. At Paso Nacional, turn right toward General Lázaro Cárdenas, which lies

*Juan de Oñate's journal began at Aguaje de la Vieja, and today a
small village at the site is called Agua Vieja. Photo by author.*

north of the Nazas. Just before entering Cárdenas, turn left and follow the signs
to San Luís Cordero and Gallo.

Lafora and Rivera both mention arriving at the Río Nazas at Hacienda San
Antonio. There is a San Antonio a few kilometers west of Paso Nacional, and this
may be the crossing point. Oñate said the crossing was at the Renteria ford, but
this location is not known. However, you must cross today by driving north from
Paso Nacional. As you drive west from Cárdenas, you will cross the streambed
of the Río Naycha. The camino was east of the Naycha's braided channel here.
Lafora crossed over the Naycha, a stream with little water and many branches, he
said, about eight kilometers (five miles) after fording the Nazas.

After you reach San Luís Cordero (gas up here), the road twists before
going due north to San Pedro del Gallo. (At KM 52, a dirt road will be on your
left that leads back to the previously visited El Casco on México 45.) Oñate, in
1597, called the location Ojo del Gallo. By the time Rivera (1724) came through,
it had become a presidio, San Pedro del Gallo. Del Gallo, Pasaje, and San
Francisco de Conchos were all begun in 1685, but by the time that Lafora was

here (1767), he noted that the presidio had been "extinguished." Del Gallo was closed in 1751, along with presidios at San Bartolomé, Cerrogordo, Mapimí, and Conchos. Their forces were replaced with a "flying squad" of seventy men head-quartered at Guajoquilla (you'll visit this site later).

Del Gallo has a nice plaza and church, with the usual array of markers pro-vided by INAH, the national archaeological and historical institute. From Del Gallo, continue north another 33 kilometers (19.8 miles) to the east-west road, where you should turn right, headed toward Mapimí. You left the camino at Del Gallo, as it turned northwest toward La Zarca, which you visited on your trip south from Parral. You'll pick up the Camino Real again at Ciudad Jiménez, the old presidial town of Guajoquilla.

Continue east, passing through Mapimí. Ruxton, for some unknown rea-son, had used an eastern route from El Gallo and passed through Mapimí in 1846. He was traveling with one companion through areas infested with Comanches, and he saw raiding parties from that tribe on several occasions. At Bermejillio you can go north on either the older free road or utilize the new toll road. Either way, go north toward Ciudad Jiménez, the next stop.

GUAJOQUILLA (CIUDAD JIMÉNEZ)

Ciudad Jiménez is situated on the Río Florido, a tributary of the Conchos. Turn left from the highway at Hidalgo, where there is a stoplight. You will see a sign to Centro. Then continue on Hidalgo until you see the plaza and church. This was the center of the presidio of Guajoquilla. If you drive a block or two behind the church, you will look down on the valley of the Río Florido. The Urrutia map will give you a clear picture of what Guajoquilla was like in 1767, some of which you can still see today. The church and plaza are intact, and the present roads are built directly on top of the older ones named in the map.

A flying squad was established here in 1751. These squads were supposed to be highly mobile and travel throughout a wide area, protecting the inhabitants. But in the Reglamento of 1772, the presidial force here was moved to the banks of the Rio Grande south of El Paso del Norte. It was first moved to San Elceario on the latitude of Carrizal, but it was soon moved again to a point a few miles south of Socorro (now in Texas). The new site, San Elizario (with change of spelling), you visited earlier.

Guajoquilla in the late 1840s was a well-established town. John Taylor Hughes, a soldier in the Doniphan expedition, noted that it had "a great number of beautiful canals, which convey water through the whole town." Ruxton had

PLAN OF THE PRESIDIO AT GUAJOQUILLA

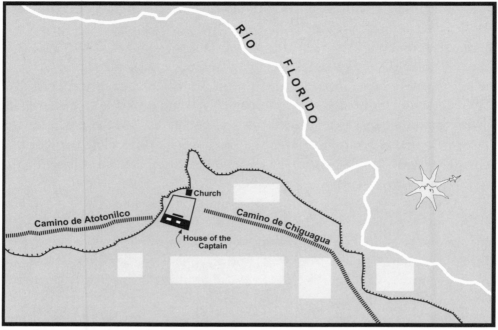

Based on a map drawn by Joseph de Urrutia in 1766

stayed in Guajoquilla a little earlier, in October 1846. While he was there, ten survivors of the band of twenty-one Americans that had separated from the Speyer-Webb caravan were brought into town. Ruxton described the men as they entered town as "miserable, emaciated creatures such as he'd never seen." They had become hopelessly lost and made it out alive only by coming across some Mexican shepherds.

Zebulon Pike, too, had traveled through Guajoquilla on his escorted tour to Louisiana. Calling it Guaxequillo in his journal, he noted that a ball was held the night he was there, with sixty women in attendance, "ten or a dozen of whom were very handsome."

To place Guajoquilla in its place on the Camino Real, we have to remember that it is on the bank of the Río Florido. The Camino Real heading south left Guajoquilla going upstream (southwest) on the Florido. The first stop was Hacienda Dolores (Ojo Dolores today), and then travelers continued up the stream, stopping at Atotonilco (now Villa López) before finally meeting up with the earlier camino at Villa Coronado, which had gone north to Valle San Bartolomé. From Villa Coronado, they left the river, heading south to Cerro Gordo (see map in chapter five).

Leave Ciudad Jiménez on México 45, the toll road, going north toward Ciudad Camargo. On this stretch, the Florido and associated farming activity will be on your right. In Ciudad Camargo, look for Chihuahua 72, the road to La Boquilla, the reservoir on the Río Conchos. Your first opportunity to turn left toward La Boquilla comes on the southern outskirts of Camargo. At about twenty kilometers (twelve miles) on this highway, turn right toward San Francisco de Conchos.

SAN FRANCISCO DE CONCHOS

San Francisco de Conchos was both a civilian community and a presidio. When Rivera passed through here in 1726, he said the pueblo was a half league to the east of the presidio and was populated by Tarahumares, Chizos, Conchos, and Tavosos. Lafora, in June 1766, noted the extinguished presidio but said there were still a few people in the pueblo. The first attempt at having a mission here, in 1645, was a failure, as two missionaries lost their lives to Conchos Indians. Today the beautiful white church is striking. The old presidio chapel is situated

The striking church at San Francisco de Conchos. The Conchos were the Conchos Indians. Photo by author.

*There was a presidio at San Francisco de Conchos, but it was
upstream about two miles from the church. The photo shows the ruins
of the presidial chapel with the cemetery behind. Photo by author.*

3.2 kilometers (1.9 miles) to the west, surrounded by a cemetery. To get to the
presidial chapel, drive two blocks to the small plaza, turn left a block and then
right, and then continue on this road (you should be parallel to the river and
going upstream) for 2.9 kilometers (1.8 miles). The cemetery and ruined adobe
chapel will be on your left.

Return to Ciudad Camargo by the same road. Camargo is a small city of
about forty thousand inhabitants situated at the confluence of the Ríos Conchos
and Florido. Such an ideal location was recognized early by the Spanish, but
Conchos and Tarahumares Indians had other ideas. Settlement by Spaniards did
not occur until 1797, when some families from San Francisco de Conchos were
moved here. Camargo was originally named Santa Rosalía and was described by
Zebulon Pike in 1807 as "a poor miserable village."

Leave Camargo on the toll road going north toward Delicias. Delicias is a new town, but nearby Meoqui and Rosales are much older. Meoqui was founded in 1712 on the Río San Pedro, while Rosales dates from 1620. Pike mentions the "Río Sn. Paubla" and presidio by the same name on his trip south in 1807, but the river was actually the San Pedro.

North of Delicias, the camino headed for Bachimba, which had a dependable source of water. Beyond Bachimba the camino went northwest through a gap in the mountains toward Mapula, now a stop on the railroad. From Mapula it was an easy entrance into Chihuahua City.

You might want to make a short detour to Aquiles Serdán, the site of the major silver discovery in 1707 that led to the development of Chihuahua city. The turn to this town comes just before you arrive in Chihuahua. Originally the mining town was called Santa Eulalia. Not a lot remains to see there today.

Continue to Chihuahua, where you have completed the tour.

Suggested Readings

Much of the literature on the Camino Real de Tierra Adentro is in Spanish and difficult to locate. The portion of the Camino Real in the United States is well covered, and many books and articles on this topic are available. The titles listed below are intended to assist the person planning to travel the camino. The enjoyment of the trip down the old camino is greatly enhanced by good preparation. And, while traveling in your car, you should have several of the books on the camino with you so you can enjoy your various stops by consulting the appropriate journal.

Many of the most important camino sites are in Mexico, and to facilitate travel there, I have included an appendix to help and encourage you to cross into that wonderful, hospitable country. The joy of standing at the river crossing in San Bartolomé (Oñate's starting point in 1598) is immeasurable. Zacatecas is yet another remarkable city, and the Oñate hacienda in nearby Pánuco is a location that brings out great emotion.

GENERAL BACKGROUND

Although several general histories have been written on the Santa Fe Trail, the Camino Real lacks such books. The books below can partly serve as a general history, but a definitive study is badly needed. Within each category below, the books or articles are arranged in order of importance as perceived by the author.

Max L. Moorehead, *New Mexico's Royal Road: Trade and Travel on the Chihuahua Trail* (University of Oklahoma Press, 1995). This fine book will make the Camino Real–Santa Fe Trail connection clear. Moorhead covers in detail the Camino Real from Chihuahua to Santa Fe and also has an extensive section on Juan de Oñate's trip north in 1598.

Marc Simmons, *The Last Conquistador: Juan de Oñate and the Settling of the Far Southwest* (University of Oklahoma Press, 1991). Simmons details the life and times of Oñate in a very readable manner. The story of Cristóbal, the father, and Juan, the son, is the story behind the Camino Real.

Josiah Gregg, *Commerce of the Prairies* (University of Oklahoma Press, 1990). This book is read principally for the story of trade on the Santa Fe Trail, but Gregg went farther south in Mexico, and his chapters on the southern reaches of the camino are invaluable.

Southern Camino Histories

Philip Wayne Powell, *Soldiers, Indians, and Silver: The Northward Advance of New Spain, 1550–1600* (University of California Press, 1952). This is the definitive story of the early development of the Camino Real. Powell describes the challenges confronting the Spaniards as they attempted to exploit the mines at Zacatecas and move the silver south to Mexico City.

Peter J. Bakewell, *Silver Mining and Society in Colonial Mexico, Zacatecas, 1546–1700* (Cambridge University Press, 1971). Bakewell carefully describes the processes involved in the silver-mining industry and also gives a good history of the city of Zacatecas, the nucleus of northward expansion.

Lloyd Mecham, *Francisco de Ibarra and Nueva Vizcaya* (Duke University Press, 1927). Mecham tells the story of expansion from Zacatecas northward into Nueva Vizcaya. Ibarra was yet another Basque involved in frontier heroics.

Robert Cooper West, *The Mining Community in Northern New Spain: The Parral Mining District* (University of California Press, 1949). West analyzes a small area in Nueva Vizcaya in a way that one understands the complexities of a mining community. The community of San Bartolomé is included in his discussion.

Oakah L. Jones, Jr., *Nueva Vizcaya: Heartland of the Spanish Frontier* (University of New Mexico Press, 1988). Jones covers Nueva Vizcaya through 1821. The northern limit of Nueva Vizcaya during the colonial period extended to just south of El Paso del Norte, so this book covers a very large section of the Camino Real.

CAMINO JOURNALS, COLONIAL PERIOD

George Hammond and Agapito Rey, eds., *Don Juan de Oñate: Colonizer of New Mexico, 1595–1628* (University of New Mexico Press, 1953). This journal is essential for camino scholars. Sections of the journal leave us wondering exactly where the camino passed, but many are crystal clear.

Gaspar Pérez de Villagrá, *Historia de Nuevo Mexico* (Mexico, D.F.: Instituto Nacional de Antropología e Historia, 1993). Villagra was a member of Oñate's expedition in 1598 and wrote the story after the fact. He is a very poetic writer and often quoted on markers in Mexico.

Charles Wilson Hackett and Charmion Clair Shelby, eds., *Revolt of the Pueblo Indians of New Mexico and Otermín's Attempted Reconquest, 1680–1682* (University of New Mexico Press, 1942). This important book is about the movement south of Otermín and the refugees after the Pueblo Revolt.

John L. Kessell and Rick Hendricks, eds., *By Force of Arms: The Journals of don Diego de Vargas, 1691–1693* (University of New Mexico Press, 1992). Interesting camino information is provided by de Vargas.

Vito Alessio Robles, *Diario y Derratero de Caminando: Visto y Observado en la visita que hizo a los Presidios de la Nueva España Septentrional el Brigadier Pedro de Rivera* (Mexico, D.F.: Taller Autográfico, 1946). This essential document gives a day-by-day account of Rivera's journey to New Mexico in 1724.

Thomas H. Naylor and Charles W. Polzer, SJ, eds., *Pedro de Rivera and the Military Regulations for Northern New Spain* (University of Arizona Press, 1988). This is another version of Rivera's trip, valuable because it is written in English and also because it discusses the outcomes of the Rivera inspection.

Eleanor B. Adams, ed., *Bishop Tamarón's Visitation of New Mexico, 1760* (University of New Mexico Press, 1954). Tamarón's story begins at Carrizal, which at the time was the southernmost community in New Mexico. Very enjoyable account of late-colonial New Mexico.

Vito Alessio Robles, ed., *Nicolás de Lafora, relación del viaje que hizo a los presidios internos, situados en la frontera de la América septentrional, perteneciemte al rey de España* (Mexico, D.F.: Editorial Pedro Robredo, 1939). Lafora was second in command to the Marqués de Rubí on Rubí's inspection of presidios from 1766 through 1767. These logs were essential in reconstructing the route of the camino in Mexico.

Lawrence Kinnaird, *The Frontiers of New Spain: Nicolás de Lafora's Description, 1766–1768* (Berkeley: Quivira Society, 1958). Kinnaird gives another version of Lafora's trip, bit it's not as detailed as previous entry.

Alfred Barnaby Thomas, *Forgotten Frontiers: A Study of the Spanish Indian Policy of don Juan Bautista de Anza, Governor of New Mexico, 1777–1787* (University of Oklahoma Press, 1932). This book tells us of de Anza's trips to the battles with the Comanches to the north and his trip south on the camino.

Elliott Coues, ed., *Zebulon M. Pike: Expeditions in the Years 1805–1806–1807* (Ross and Haines, 1965). There are two good versions of the Pike expedition, but Coues details Pike's route south of Colorado state while the second does not. Pike went south as far as Guajoquilla before being taken to Monclova and Texas.

Camino Journals, Postcolonial

Adolph Wislizenus, MD, *Memoirs of a Tour to Northern Mexico* (Calvin Horn, 1969). This journal is full of adventure since Wislizenus was traveling with Albert Speyer, who was carrying two wagons of rifles for the governor of Chihuahua. They managed to just stay ahead of a pursuing U.S. force. Wislizenus was exiled in Cusihuiriáchic until the battle of Sacramento had concluded.

James Josiah Webb, *Adventures in the Santa Fe Trade, 1844–1847* (University of Nebraska Press, 1995). Webb was another trader in Chihuahua and beyond during the Mexican War period. This story lets the reader know how the trade was carried out in Mexico.

George Frederick Ruxton, *Adventures in Mexico and the Rocky Mountains, 1846–1847* (Rio Grande Press, 1973). If one were to read only one book about the camino, this might be it. Ruxton traveled north from Mexico

City in 1846, passing through every important site. He has firsthand
accounts of Armijo, Speyer, and Kirker.

John Taylor Hughes, *Doniphan's Expedition, 1847* (Texas A & M Press, 1997).
Many of the soldiers in Doniphan's expedition wrote journals about
their experiences, but this one by Hughes is among the best.

Stella M. Drumm, ed., *Down the Santa Fe Trail and into Mexico: The Diary
of Susan Shelby Magoffin* (University of Nebraska Press, 1982). This
classic account is usually read by Santa Fe Trail devotees, but it is
worthwhile for Magoffin's comments on the Camino Real as well.

General Interest

John Roney, "Tracing the Camino Real: The Chihuahua Section," in *El
Camino Real de Tierra Adentro*, compiled by Gabrielle Palmer (BLM:
Cultural Resource Series #11, 1993). Roney does a thorough job of
describing the camino in Chihuahua state. This report was based on
extensive fieldwork in the area.

Phillip Wayne Powell, "The Forty-Niners of Sixteenth Century Mexico,"
Pacific Historical Review 19 (August 1950): 235–49. Powell makes some
interesting comparisons between gold rush Californians and the early
miners of Mexico.

Max Moorhead, *The Presidio: Bastion of the Spanish Borderland* (University
of Oklahoma Press, 1975). Presidios were an important aspect of
Spanish colonial strategy, and Moorhead does a very nice job of
outlining successes and failures of the policy.

Max Moorhead, *The Apache Frontier: Jacobo Ugarte and Spanish-Indian
Relations in Northern New Spain, 1769–1791* (University of Oklahoma
Press, 1968). The Apaches were the scourge in the northern portions
of the camino territory, and Moorhead tells how the Spanish attempted
to control them.

Rex E. Gerald, *Spanish Presidios in the Late Eighteenth Century in Northern
New Spain* (Museum of New Mexico, 1968). This work includes Gerald's
research on the Carrizal presidio south of El Paso.

Fray Angélico Chávez, *Origins of New Mexico Families: A Genealogy of the Spanish Colonial Period* (Museum of New Mexico, 1974). Chávez does a very thorough job of researching the many families in early New Mexico.

C. Brooks, *Complete History of the Mexican War* (Rio Grande Press, 1965). Brooks gives background for the battles at Brazito, Sacramento, and Mexico City.

Elinore M. Barrett, *Conquest and Catastrophe: Changing Rio Grande Pueblo Settlement Patterns in the Sixteenth and Seventeenth Centuries* (University of New Mexico Press, 2002). Barrett does a superb job of telling the story of the impact of the Spanish conquest on the Pueblo Indians. The title of her book tells it all.

Clara Bargellini, *Historia y Arte en un pueblo rural: San Bartolomé, hoy Valle de Allende, Chihuahua* (Mexico: Universidad Nacional Autónoma de México, Instituto de Investigaciónes Estéticas, 1998). This is a good source for those going to Oñate's starting place, San Bartolomé.

Herman Agoyo and Lynwood Brown, eds., *When Cultures Meet: Remembering San Gabriel del Yungue Oweene* (Sunstone Press, 1987). Oñate's first capital is covered in detail, with nice photos provided of the excavations under way at the time, since filled in.

Christine Preston, *The Royal Road: El Camino Real from Mexico City to Santa Fe* (University of New Mexico Press, 1998). This photo-essay on the camino has superb photos.

Bernal Díaz del Castillo, *The Discovery and Conquest of Mexico* (Noonday Press, 1968). Bernal Díaz was a soldier in Cortés's invading army. His account of the conquest is one of the very best.

SUGGESTIONS FOR TRAVEL IN MEXICO

In this appendix, I hope to encourage you to visit the portion of the Camino Real that lies in Mexico. This section forms by far the greater part of the camino and contains a substantial number of very important sites. In particular, I think that those readers interested in the travels of Juan de Oñate would certainly like to travel south to get a feel for his challenges and accomplishments.

The first hurdle to overcome is that of consideration for your personal safety. As I write this appendix from my home in the Albuquerque metropolitan area, I will tell you that at least fifteen homicides occurred here in the past month (five in one day alone). I don't think that this fact will keep many visitors away from Albuquerque. Our national press covers Mexico in some detail and especially the homicides in border zones. I fully recognize the ongoing tragedy in Ciudad Juárez, with so many young women being murdered, but I suggest that you will be safe when you visit Mexico. The only large city you will visit is Mexico City, where you are advised to use taxis, as I do when I visit that megalopolis. I choose taxis not for personal safety but because that city is so difficult to drive in.

As for highway safety, the roads in Mexico are as good as ours. Much of your travel will be on four-lane divided highways with tolls that keep most traffic off these highways because of the cost. Additionally, highways in Mexico are patrolled by Ángeles Verdes, Green Angels, who use special trucks (painted green, of course) to help any traveler in trouble. The days of burros sleeping on the roads are pretty much a thing of the past.

To enter Mexico and journey beyond the border city of Ciudad Juárez, you will need a passport and your car title, and you will want to purchase Mexican auto insurance. A birth certificate can substitute for the passport. The passport is necessary for you to obtain a tourist card (good for six months) for about twenty dollars, payable at almost any bank in the republic. If you have flown to Mexico, you paid this fee as part of your airfare.

You will need a temporary import permit for your car, and that is why you need the original car title, not a copy. The car, by the way, must be yours free and clear or you'll need a letter from the company holding the lien on the car giving their permission for you to take the car out of this country.

Your auto insurance is probably valid only within a short distance of the border, so you will want insurance valid in Mexico. There are agents in every border town specializing in such insurance. I buy mine in Albuquerque, at Associated Insurance Professionals, 1429 Carlisle. Their phone number is (505) 265-3704. You can get Mexican insurance at any AAA office as well. You will be charged by the number of days you will be in Mexico and the value of your car wherever you purchase it. There are also two agencies in El Paso: one is Sanborns, the other Las Palmas.

I am asked constantly why we have to go through all this, since we are Americans and the Mexicans want us as tourists. Remember, the tourist card is much like a visa. Imagine yourself a Mexican citizen standing in a two-block-long line serpentining around the American Embassy in Mexico City. This line is a daily event for Mexicans seeking a visa to visit the United States. Now you should realize the ten minutes or so necessary for you to obtain your tourist card isn't so onerous.

The permit for your car is a bit more difficult to explain. Mexico has an automobile industry, and the government therefore wants Mexican citizens to purchase cars produced in Mexico. Unfettered entrance of American-owned cars into Mexico would seriously injure the Mexican auto industry by flooding the country with inexpensive used cars. Your car permit costs about twenty dollars and must be paid with a credit card. You have six months in which to return the car to a border station, where your car will be officially "checked out" of Mexico.

You may recall that I suggest in the text that you utilize the new border crossing west of Juárez to enter Mexico. It's across from Santa Teresa, New

Mexico. You can now obtain both your tourist card and car import license at this station, which is hardly used, so lines are few. It also allows you to avoid Ciudad Juárez entirely, as the road south from here misses the city.

GENERAL TRAVEL SUGGESTIONS

Much of the time, you will be driving on modern toll roads (four lanes, divided). These highways are patrolled by the Green Angels trucks in case you need help. Gasoline is sold at Pemex stations, Pemex being Petróleos Mexicanos, a government monopoly. Prices are almost identical at all the Pemex stations, so there is no reason to shop around. These stations are ubiquitous, but it is always a good idea to drive on the top half of your tank. The unit of measure for gasoline is the liter (about four liters is a U.S. gallon). Mexicans have been paying over $2.50 per gallon for years, so don't expect any sympathy from them for high prices.

Maps and Guides
In the text, I mentioned that the best road maps are by Guia Roji. These are available at the several Sanborns restaurants along the camino route. (Note: Sanborns insurance company is not the same.) The map available through AAA is almost worthless for our purpose. I also use the maps sold by INEGI, the Mexican government agency that maps the country. INEGI is the Mexican equivalent of the United States Geological Survey (USGS). INEGI has outlets in all major cities, and I have listed the addresses of the INEGI outlets along our route. If you can get to the library at the University of New Mexico (Centennial Library), which has almost all the INEGI maps, you can photocopy those maps you need.

INEGI *Addresses*
    Ciudad Juárez: Av. Plutarco Elías Calles No. 951 Norte
        Colonia Progresista, CP 32310
    Chihuahua: Av. Technológico No. 2907
        Col. Magisterial, CP 31310
    Durango: Blvd. Heroico Colegio Militár No. 444 Oriente
        Col. Santa Fé, CP 34240
    Zacatecas: Av. Hidalgo No. 626
        Centro Histórico
    Querétaro: Av. Constituyentes, esquina con Av. Pasteur S/N
        Col. Centro CP 76000

Distrito Federal: Balderas No. 71
Col. Centro, Delegación Cuauhtémoc, CP 06040
(this is but one of many INEGI outlets in the capital)

Guidebooks

The best guide of Mexico for camino travelers is published by Lonely Planet. It covers all the medium-size and most of the small cities along our route. Once again, AAA has a guide, but it does not cover all the necessary towns and lists expensive hotels only. Get Lonely Planet!

Hotels and Restaurants

I will follow the basic route that I used in the text to suggest hotels I have utilized or ones that appear to be satisfactory. I generally do not stay in expensive hotels, and you should know that in advance. At several locations along the way, you may find yourself in small communities that do not have very fancy hotels, so be warned. A very good source of hotel information is found at the Web site allmexicohotels.com.

VILLA AHUMADA: Hotel del Camino, south end of town on the right. A decent restaurant is the Arizona. It is on the right as you enter town from the north. There is an ATM machine across the railroad tracks at a bank in the center of town.

CHIHUAHUA: I stay at El Campanario on Boulevard Díaz Ordaz, an easy walk to the plaza and restaurants. A good restaurant is La Mesquite, about two blocks from the hotel. Ask the person at the desk for directions.

HIDALGO DEL PARRAL: I always stay at Los Arcos, on Dr. Pedro de Lille, which is adjacent to the bus station and one block off Independencia. The hotel has a decent restaurant as well.

VALLE DE ALLENDE: Rita Soto, the town historian, has a nice B and B on Mina. Ask anyone for directions to Rita's.

DURANGO: I have stayed at the Hotel Roma, which is just one block off the plaza and very near the Sanborns restaurant.

ZACATECAS: Best bet here is the Condesa on Juárez. It is an easy walk to the cathedral and near several good restaurants. If you have some spare change, eat dinner at the restaurant in the Quinta Real hotel. This hotel is built around the old bull ring, and sitting at your table, you will look down on the ring and up at the old aqueduct. A bit expensive but well worth it.

Dolores Hidalgo: The hotel El Caudillo is very near the main church. Good rooms with a bit of bell ringing to remind you that are in Padre Hidalgo's town. The hotel has a good restaurant.

San Miguel Allende: There are dozens of choices, all a bit more expensive than elsewhere for the same-quality room. You might try the four-star La Aldea, which is three blocks from the Jardín and across from the Instituto Allende.

Querétaro: The Amberes on Corregidora is a good choice here.

Mexico City: When I don't stay with friends, I stay at the Bristol. It is on Plaza Necaxa, about two blocks behind the American Embassy. A commercial, no-frills hotel with good rates for Mexico City, an easy walk to Reforma and the Pink Zone. Another old favorite is the Majestic Hotel, directly on the zócalo. It is worth visiting the Majestic bar on the top floor just to look down on the beautiful zócalo.

Cuencamé: This is a small town but the only place to stay if you wish to explore the old presidio town Pasaje nearby. La Posta Inn Hotel is on the north end of Gral. Severino Ceniceros at No. 68 Norte. The owner can direct you to a restaurant back in town.

Ciudad Jiménez: Las Pampas Motel is on the Carretera Jiménez-Chihuahua about one kilometer out of town. This is the only stop between Gómez Palacio and Ciudad Camargo, and you probably will stay here to visit this presidio town of Guajoquilla.

Ciudad Camargo: On the south end of town as you enter (on the left) is a very nice motel called the Santa Fé, which has good rooms and a good restaurant. The road to San Francisco de Conchos is just beyond the hotel.

Index

Page numbers in **bold type** indicate maps;
page numbers in *italic type* indicate illustrations.